Kate Chopin's *The Awakening*

Kate Chopin's
THE AWAKENING

Screenplay as Interpretation

Marilyn Hoder-Salmon

University Press of Florida
Gainesville Tallahassee Tampa Boca Raton
Pensacola Orlando Miami Jacksonville

Frontispiece. Mary Fairchild MacMonnies Low, *Five O'Clock Tea* (1891). The artist's life holds striking parallels to Kate Chopin's. She lived in New Orleans and St. Louis, where at the School of Fine Arts she led a rebellion for women to draw from the nude. Few of her impressionist works survived because her second husband, envious and controlling, lost a collection of her paintings on tour. By permission of the Sheldon Swope Art Museum, Terre Haute, Indiana.

Copyright 1992 by the Board of Regents of the State of Florida
Printed in the United States of America on acid-free paper ♾
All rights reserved

Library of Congress Cataloging in Publication Data appear on the last printed page of the book.

The University Press of Florida is the scholarly publishing agency of the State University System of Florida, comprised of Florida A & M University, Florida Atlantic University, Florida International University, Florida State University, University of Central Florida, University of Florida, University of North Florida, University of South Florida, and University of West Florida.

University Press of Florida
15 Northwest 15th Street
Gainesville, FL 32611

To Melinda, Randye, and Mike

CONTENTS

PREFACE

All translation is an interpretation, an explication of a beloved text.
Justin O'Brien
"The French Literary Horizon"

Wouldn't Kate Chopin, herself a remarkable interpreter of irony, destiny, and intuition, have relished the multiple ironies of that day in 1945, as I have imagined it, when French professor Cyrille Arnavon wandered into a Paris bookshop and laid hands on a half-century-old copy of her novel *The Awakening*? What if instead of taking the musty book over to the cashier, he had just skimmed a few pages and set the slender novel back on the shelf or table where it had rested for so long? Think of the impoverishment to the project of rediscovery of the heritage of important fiction by women writers! But of course he did take the book and for a few francs set in motion the evolution of what has become an essential ingredient in feminist literary history. Now, along with scores of readers and critics, I claim the novel as a "beloved text."

As someone trained in interdisciplinary studies, I am not surprised when, often with no plan in mind, I find myself pursuing new interests; however, I surely could not have anticipated where my preoccupation with Kate Chopin's nineteenth-century novel would one day lead. With *The Awakening* as centerpiece I have undertaken to bring together elements of adaptation studies, feminist literary and film criticism, women's social history of the late nineteenth century in Louisiana, screenplay writing, and more. Perhaps here is the place to say then, that a little risk venturing, a little patience, and a lot of trust may be required of readers of this study. What I've done is take my parallel interests in interdisciplinary and comparative studies and blend them to construct a different way to analyze literature. Screenplay writing is the methodology.

Teachers of literature and film are using fiction-into-film studies with increasing frequency to teach and write about the interconnections of and differences between prose and cinema. This approach, many academics agree, illuminates fiction and film and, in enhancing our comprehension of both arts, helps to lessen the separation between media. The availability in recent times of published screenplays of adaptations is facilitating work in fiction-into-film studies. My study takes the genre a step further by illustrating that a critic or a student may adapt fiction, not to be made into a film, but to use the process of adaptation as a critical methodology itself, undertaking the adaptation as an interpretation of the original source. It is perhaps the ultimate step in following current critical injunctions to "enter the text" in order to unmask its mysteries. This book is my case study of this idea.

I am drawn to Chopin's protagonist, Edna Pontellier, because her search for an uncompromising autonomy in the late nineteenth century, while a rare portrayal for the times, resonates with even greater clarity and purpose almost a century later for today's woman. The restrictive apparel of Chopin's era disappeared long ago, but women are still hobbled by patriarchal tradition and still seek an autonomous identity. A great part of my motivation, therefore, to embark on this study lies in my long-term fascination with Chopin's novel and my correspondent desire to more fully comprehend its enigmas. Certainly the prolific and interesting criticism of *The Awakening* had aided but had not completely satisfied this compelling interest.

As I have peripherally indicated, and as I will elaborate in the Backgrounds chapter, many contexts brought me to this idea. The absence of adaptations of feminist fiction in film provided some part of the inspiration for my inquiry into the intersections of fiction-into-film studies and feminist criticism. I could not help but note the singular lack of attention in feminist film criticism to the omission from the film canon of films based on significant women's literature, and the reductive treatment when the rare film based on such classics was made. The adaptation literature, which is really quite extensive, has little to offer the feminist critic. Because such a large percentage of Hollywood films was based on fictional sources, and because the histories of women in fiction and of women in film have many parallels, this critical oversight seemed worth noting. A theme of fiction-into-film criticism is the reductive treatment the Hollywood film industry tended to apply to most fictional sources regardless of perspective. The almost uniform stripping away of feminist content is notable in that it left the audience of the most powerful media of the twentieth century bereft of authentic female roles from original sources. Patriarchal stereotypes are the dominant themes and characterizations.

Simple logistics preclude the restoration of almost a century of omission. The recovery of women's fiction, as dramatic as it may be, is still largely a project of the academy rather than a popular trend. And feminist filmmakers, largely outside the Hollywood mainstream, tend to produce documentaries and avant-garde films. The lack of a literature in feminist criticism of adaptation studies ought to have led me into my own study of film adaptation and women's fiction, but I took a different tack. I grew fascinated by the idea of transposing an authentic and complex portrayal of a woman's character and theme into a cinematic form as illustration that it both could and ought to be done. Since I am not a filmmaker, the idea of writing a screenplay became an accessible project and led to further revelations, which I will discuss later. I only want to suggest here that as I undertook to adapt a nineteenth-century novel into a twentieth-century screenplay, I became convinced that calling attention through this process to the loss to film and to society of the heritage of women's fiction is worthwhile.

As I have noted, both absences and ideas in feminist literature and film history and in criticism led me into this project. But along the way, deeply engrossed by the process, I came gradually to yet another realization. Often, as literature and film devotees, we wish to test our own creative ability; the impulse is active, but we remain hesitant to take the first step, or, as teachers, we may seek to develop students' creative tendencies. Screenplay writing, I discovered, provides a secure avenue for experimenting with creative potential and for exercising imaginative capacities. Screenplay format is not difficult to learn, and there are many manuals readily available (a select few are listed in the bibliography). In translating an original story to a visual analogue the adapter is free to alter, add, subtract, and otherwise transform the source as narrative prose is adapted to filmic structure and language. Such intimate contact with both arts may uncover ideas about theme, plot, point of view, characterization, setting, interiority, and other prose and filmic devices that resist analysis through more typical means. In adaptation one is working with the creation of an accomplished author. The proximity to the mind and methods of the original author that adaptation fosters should provide a learning experience that literature and film students would find instructive and engrossing. One can learn a great deal about how writers write, as well as hone one's own expressive writing skills. Screenplays can be elegant, even poetic.

As part of the critical process of such an undertaking, a particular critical mode should accompany the analysis to provide a focus for interpretation, such as psychoanalysis, semiotics, or feminist criticism. Furthermore, if the original source is a work removed from our own time, then a review of the historical background necessary to create setting certainly helps to locate the work in its time and place.

Of course, a one-semester course does not allow a student the time to attempt an adaptation of a novel, as I have done for this study. Instead a chapter, a short story, a poem, or an act of a play may be selected to transpose into scenes or sequences. In my teaching, which is usually in women's studies courses, I find that students saturated with term papers welcome innovative assignments.

I hope to show that as an intellectual and imaginative exercise to interpret literature and film, adaptation offers an opportunity for experimentation that takes one deeper into both arts. The plan of this study is as follows: The screenplay is bracketed by two essays. The first is a backgrounds chapter in which I briefly discuss masculine/feminine themes in film, adaptation theory, Kate Chopin's life, and *The Awakening*'s unique history to illustrate how I came to this idea and to introduce the intellectual strands that inform my project. I use the question of women's search for autonomy as a thematic unity that connects Chopin's life and work to relationships between the social history of the time and our time and to feminist criticism. The resulting new work, which retains the essential themes and complexities of *The Awakening*, is intended as an analogue of the novel. The screenplay, titled *Edna*, is in three acts. An interpretive chapter follows, in which I show how the conventions of fiction into film—image, time, setting, characterization, interiority, and dialogue, for example—are employed to develop the central ideas of the screenplay. If some readers are led to—or back to—Chopin's novel, I will be very pleased.

ACKNOWLEDGMENTS

From start to finish the intellectual and personal support of many institutions and people accompanied me through this study. Evelyn Helmick was one of the first scholars to teach Kate Chopin's singular novel, and I'll always be in her debt for that long-ago awakening. Much is owed to Mary Power, ardent Joycean and wonderful mentor and friend. For all my cherished memories of excellent teaching and inspired parties, I thank her. At a time when some branded my study "too unconventional," several mentors, then all at the University of New Mexico, gave me encouragement and advice, and I particularly want to thank them—George Arms, Hamlin Hill, Ira Jaffe, and Sam Girgus.

The facilities and staff of four libraries aided my research: the Zimmerman Library at University of New Mexico, the Howard-Tilton Memorial Library at Tulane University, the Otto G. Richter Library at University of Miami, and the University Libraries of Florida International University. I also wish to thank the staff of the Missouri Historical Society, the Newcomb College Center for Research on Women, and the National Museum of Women's Art.

At Florida International University many of my women's studies colleagues have supported my endeavors. I especially want to thank Joyce Peterson, and I cannot say which I value most, her friendship or her example. And to Gail Massey, a special thank you for being a joy to work with. I would also like to thank John Stack and Tom Breslin for their support. The University Press of Florida associates have my highest praise; I got to know Walda Metcalf the best, and I thank her the most.

The Davenports deserve my thanks for loaning me their Sanibel Island home for a summer so I could write the first draft of the screenplay in seclusion and in the appropriate atmosphere. For perfect friendship I thank Maxine Thurston. And I thank my parents, Mitch and Fran Fleisher, who have seen me through many transitions.

Finally, I acknowledge my debt to my daughters, Melinda and Randye, who have given me many a remarkable moment, but never a dull one. And to Mike, who married into a melodrama and learned to play his part with wisdom and grace.

BACKGROUNDS

Re-vision—the act of looking back, of seeing with fresh eyes, of entering an old text from a new critical direction—is for women more than a chapter in cultural history: it is an act of survival. Until we can understand the assumptions in which we are drenched, we cannot know ourselves.
Adrienne Rich
"On Lies, Secrets, and Silence"

Three esteemed human characteristics—creativity, interpretation, and connection—undergird the impetus for both the act of criticism and the act of adaptation. The synthesis of these two modes, criticism and adaptation, forms a compelling frontier, as many academics have found, in literature and film studies. Within the genre is a byway, only rarely explored, wherein the commonalities of creativity, interpretation, and connection form an analogical, if unique, alliance. In this study I go beyond the customary methodologies of fiction-into-film studies and illustrate why and how an original adaptation of an important precursor, undertaken specifically for interpretive purposes, may in itself represent a viable form of interpretation. This new approach commingles criticism and adaptation.

When an interviewer asked playwright Harold Pinter, author of screenplays based on novels by such diverse writers as Marcel Proust and John Fowles, his purpose in becoming an adapter, Pinter replied that the technical demands were challenging, but primarily he found it interesting "to enter into another [artist's] mind . . . to try to find the true mind."[1] The terminology of adaptation literature—words such as *reassemble, ingest, core, transform, essence, breakthrough,* and *synthesis*—suggests the almost biological intention of one who studies an original work in order to adapt it. To put this another way, the process of adapting significant precursors may be compared to that of archaeology, probing (excavating) deeply to uncover the mysteries of a particular text. Adaptation takes one inside the work, allowing a clinical intellectual metamorphosis to happen through which the

1

adapter may come to know the work as closely as possible. As a case study, I offer a creative enterprise, the cinematic adaptation of *The Awakening*, as a form of criticism of the novel. Because of the interdisciplinary nature of this project, as well as its novelty, I want to interweave the background for the components of my methodology with the history of how I came to this idea.

FEMALE/MALE; LITERATURE/FILM

During a summer seminar on classics of American film I observed an absence of women in the films we studied, except for a few unflattering stereotypes. Although it was not a requisite of the seminar, most of the films were adaptations, such as Orson Welles's film of Booth Tarkington's *The Magnificent Ambersons*. All the films were about masculine experience. Given that more than half of all films are based on literary sources, I became curious about the representation in film of fiction by and about women, and about the way in which Hollywood treated these sources. I began to seek out films based on fiction by women authors. The first film I viewed, *Little Women*, was representative of what I was to find. What had become of the feisty Jo I remembered from a girlhood acquaintance with Louisa May Alcott's classic? Many films later, a pattern emerged. Most films based on women's stories with even a jot of feminist theme or characterization retained little trace of their original feminist content in their cinematic versions.

Before this my sole work in film consisted of a social history of Mary McDougal Axelson's play *Life Begins* and its subsequent film history. Axelson, a 1930s playwright, wrote this dramatic story about her own experience of maternity and childbirth. The film of *Life Begins*, starring Loretta Young, opened in 1932 to mixed reviews.[2] Critics recommended the film while objecting to the "indelicacy" of the subject and claimed that only women, and then out of "morbid curiosity," would like the film. The controversy grew heated, with some reviewers calling for a law to prohibit "pictures of this type," but the public continued to buy tickets for *Life Begins*.

Many films in fact have been based on fiction by women writers, although not necessarily feminist in any way. The majority of adaptations, however, are of novels authored by men, guided into films by men. Historically, American films were rooted in Victorian-era ideology, glorifying woman as icon, adored for her beauty, her wifely self-sacrifice, and her maternal devotion. The only other available role, woman as evil incarnate who must be punished for transgressing, served as a warning to uphold proper womanhood. The disregard for authentic women's themes in film follows the pattern of the historical reception of women's fiction. It is only in the last two decades that the work of many of the neglected and undervalued women writers of earlier periods has been rediscovered, reprinted, and reinterpreted for an eager and appreciative audience.

Invariably, regardless of the degree of feminist ideas and content in novels chosen for adaptation, Hollywood has reduced their themes in translation, denying or trivializing women's experience. This is not to say that no Hollywood film has depicted women as symbols of respect, accomplishment, and truth. Feminist film critics are recovering the work of women film directors and providing new critiques that locate positive portrayals of women and of feminist themes in traditional films. It remains true, however, that most films based on both classic and popular novels reflect masculine values, culture, and myth.

Leslie Fiedler's well-known passage about the predominant American literary motif defines this content: "A man on the run, harried into the forest and out to sea, down the river or into combat—anywhere to avoid 'civilization', which is to say, the confrontation of a man and woman which leads to the fall of sex, marriage, and responsibility." Fiedler, it can be certain, had in mind such popular literary classics, which are also films, as *The Virginian, Moby-Dick, The Last of the Mohicans, Sea-Wolf, The Adventures of Tom Sawyer, The Ox-Bow Incident,* and *Billy Budd.* Recasting Fiedler's literary theme for cinema, Molly Haskell states: "The flight from women and the fight against them in their role as entrappers and civilizers is one of the major themes of American cinema."[3]

Film adaptations of women's fiction tend to illustrate the fear of women as equals. Alcott's *Little Women* provides an interesting example for several reasons: the classic novel is a rare role model for young girls; there are three adaptations; and the films are often shown on television and thereby still exert an influence. The exceptional exuberance of Jo and her success as a writer are just two elements by which the dilution of character can be gauged in both the 1933 version and the 1949 remake. In both films the tomboyish Jo is made to look unappealing, and her later achievements are minimized. The sums make the point. In the novel Jo sells her first story on her own initiative for the then magnificent fee of $100; in the 1933 film she is paid $1.50; in the 1949 version she earns $1.00, and the professor assumes control over a subdued Jo who seeks his publishing advice. This diminished spirit shows up in the characterization of Jo in the 1981 remake for television. In an essay on the *Little Women* films, Kate Ellis comments that "the problem of both these attributes [independence and earning power] is that our culture views them as masculine qualities."[4]

Less often noted but equally vexing is the reductive treatment accorded to male authors with self-expressive female characters in their fiction. Sinclair Lewis's *Main Street* offers a prototype illustration. The change of title to *I Married a Doctor* is a symbolic, if amusing, hint of the transformation of Lewis's serious reformer, Carol Kennicott, to a vapid charmer. Lewis's Carol is an intelligent and determined character who strives to achieve greater independence and fulfillment within the bonds of marriage and motherhood. In the film the city-bred Carol uses her energy to combat the envy of the town women who resent her sophistication. The novel's ending is ambiguous, with Carol reflecting on her limited choices, while the film's ending depicts her as a dutiful wife come to her senses.

Many Victorian-era European novels, especially well-known classics, were also subjected to Hollywood's domestication. Geoffrey Wagner analyzed three such adaptations, Emily Brontë's *Wuthering Heights*, Charlotte Brontë's *Jane Eyre*, and Gustave Flaubert's *Madame Bovary*. Wagner illustrates the omission of Charlotte Brontë's theme of equality and the relentless stripping away of Jane Eyre's intellect. In his chapter on Vincent Minelli's 1949 film of *Madame Bovary*, Wagner brings out each nuance of the systematic loss of feminism from the original. Moreover, in a complete inversion Charles Bovary becomes "Emma's victim rather than the cause of her suffering."[5] Further difficulties occur in these three adaptations because the fictional

symbols are faithfully transferred to the screen while the characterizations undergo a dramatic transformation, demolishing the novels' coherence between the characters and their milieu.

There are many excessive examples. The historical record weighs
heavily against fair treatment of women's themes and characterizations in most adaptations. However, fiction films have been made
that illustrate that it is possible to change this pattern and still satisfy
both the economic needs of the industry and the entertainment needs
of the audience. Often these films are from the non-American market. A film from Rainer Werner Fassbinder, based on the nineteenth-
century novel *Effi Briest* by Theodor Fontane, successfully retains
and even enhances the novel's social relevance, while re-creating a
seemingly authentic nineteenth-century milieu. The plot tells the
tragic story of Effi, a young woman who obliges her parents and
marries a pedantic Prussian more than twice her age. They return to
his village, which is alien to Effi's urban background. Soon bored by
her purposeless existence, she drifts into a brief, emotionless affair
with a local womanizer. Her husband learns of the affair seven years
later, and Effi's downfall begins as she is punished and shunned by
all, including her child. Effi has a physical breakdown, declines, and
soon dies.

Stanley Kauffmann's review notes that the character of Effi lacks
the "tragic dimensions of Emma Bovary or of Kate Chopin's Edna
because Effi is much more a victim than a rebel."[6] While I agree with
his praise of the screenplay as a "small marvel of selection, distilla-
tion, and arrangement," I maintain that Effi is subversively uncom-
pliant. Her efforts at rebellion are conducted on that small scale
common to women's revolt, so subtle that at times it may escape
notice. Fassbinder creates superb visual analogues from his literary
source to portray those small acts of resistance. One memorable
scene shows Effi as she swings back and forth, her parents and her
suitor standing together in the distance. The swing is a successful
analogy to Effi's predicament. She clings to the freedom of girlhood
as she flies toward us in innocence; as she swings back into the
shadows, it is a foreboding of her coming maturity as a wife. This
dialectic is sustained by the image of Effi's face, on which the conflict
between inner and outer self is visible: she smiles, but her eyes are
expressionless. Another example is Effi's deathbed insistence that

her maiden name be placed on her gravestone; this is her way of indicating that her real growth, as well as her hopes for the future, ended with her marriage. Traditionally women's lives as adjuncts to men are immortalized by their grave markers: "Wife of," "Daughter of," and so on. Fassbinder's film incorporates a literary style, using letters, diaries, and titles both to support the mise-en-scène and to act as ironic counterpoints to contemporary feminism. The viewer is left with the impression that very little has changed since 1894.

Exceptions aside, as I have noted, cinematic translations of films based on literary sources, regardless of the perspective of the original, generally dilute their complex and controversial themes. The record of weakening or distorting themes and characters from fiction with even a modicum of feminism, let alone from works with pronounced feminist themes, is well known. The lack of authentic female role models and stories in film will only be rectified when greater attention is given to the full cost to society of this absence. Feminist literary and film scholars are engaged in the effort, independently but with common goals, to restore women's art and experience, and to chart new ways of being female in our society. These scholars are also documenting the predominance of masculine themes and analyzing the distortion of women in literature and film.

Feminist literary criticism paved the way for feminist film criticism. Issues such as a distinctive women's style and a commitment to authenticity and equality, for example, overlap in both disciplines. Reevaluating the canon and formulating new methodologies are preoccupations of research in both literature and film studies. Also, in recent times we have witnessed a rather dramatic rise in the production by women of feminist films outside the mainstream, particularly of documentaries and avant-garde films. Together, feminist filmmakers and critics seek to explore the parameters of male dominance/female powerlessness and to give women an authentic space in cinema through honest, significant, innovative, and edgy interpretations of women's culture and experience. Feminist film criticism ranges over a diverse set of methodologies, encompassing psychoanalysis, semiotics, and Marxist ideology, and in most cases, creating inventive and dynamic ideas.

Important studies of feminist film criticism first appeared in the early 1970s. For example, Joan Mellen and Molly Haskell wrote about the social history of women in film and Claire Johnston and Laura Mulvey wrote theoretical essays that in a sense formed the foundation of the new criticism. Mellen focused the social activist nature of feminist filmmaking: "As women have been so profoundly diminished by their history (as it has been written), their stake in self-discovery and contingent social change is great. A cinema which captures this will offer much." Correspondingly, Haskell noted the relationship between women's cultural roles and their depiction in film, offering a literature/film dichotomy: "Movie heroines are viscerally immediate and accountable to audiences in a way that the heroines of literature, highbrow or popular, are not" (12). In a discussion of the rare "distinguished women's films," Haskell concludes, they take the women "out of defeat and passivity and collective identity into the radical adventure of the solitary soul, out of contrivances of puritanical thinking into enlightened self-interest" (162). Laura Mulvey, in an often reprinted essay, suggests: "The first blow against the monolithic accumulation of traditional film conventions is to free the look of the camera into its materiality in time and space and the look of the audience into dialectics, passionate detachment." At about the same time, in a well-known study of director Dorothy Arzner, Claire Johnston wrote: "The need for oppressed people to write their own history cannot be over stressed. Memory, an understanding of struggles of the past and a sense of one's own history constitute a vital dynamic in any struggle." These progenitors were followed by critics who are exploring new territory, and who include Teresa de Lauretis, Ruby Rich, Julia Lesage, E. Anne Kaplan, Judith Mayne, and Lucy Fischer, some of whom I discuss later.[7]

Given the proliferation of feminist film criticism, surprisingly little attention has been given to the omission from the Hollywood cinema of classics of women's literature and the counterpart phenomenon of reductive treatment when such classics are adapted. I believe that between the preoccupations of analyzing "the male gaze" and championing the countercinema, women's fiction-into-film history is overlooked as a category.

Why not attempt, I began to ask myself, as an exercise with many disparate but compatible strands, a cinematic translation of a precursor novel to illustrate by an original case study the elements in literature, film, culture, and theory that interest me? Although one was not likely thus to rectify almost a century of omission and distortion, several useful outcomes seemed possible. With such an exercise one might bolster the idea that women's literary heritage is worthy of a cinematic tradition, illustrate by example that it is possible to transpose a feminist literary classic to cinematic form without losing its complex integrity, and encourage filmmakers to undertake the recovery for cinema of women's rediscovered literary antecedents. Finally, experiencing an integral aspect of adaptation, reconceptualizing a "beloved text" in a new form, might deepen one's own and others' pleasure in and understanding of the original.

It seems to me, in relation to this idea, that an area where feminist film critics can apply current interests to looking back at women's literature is in the application of intertextuality to adaptation. For example, in *Shot/Countershot* Lucy Fischer, in another context, points to one possible connection: "Contemporary criticism has reformulated the notion of literary history as a dynamic interplay of texts, and the feminist critic who focuses on the creations of female artists must yet decide how to position them, what intertextual network to assume." Similarly, Judith Mayne comments on female authorship in the cinema as offering "complex textual and cultural processes which dramatize and foreground women's relationship to language, plot and the institutions of literature." She continues, "The paradigm of female authorship may provide a useful point of departure to examine the status of female authorship in the cinema."[8]

A start in this direction may be found in Ruby Rich's influential essay on "naming," in which she ventures five categories of experimental names for film genres. One of Rich's categories is based on her observation that "the tradition of realism in the cinema has never done well by women." She proposes a new realism, "Corrective Realism," for films that transform the "characteristics and the narrative workings of traditional realism" while accepting many cinematic conventions. Although the tendency in feminist film studies is to question how a feminist discourse can be articulated within a patriarchal industry, the issue is far from resolved. As Robin Wood points out, "It remains unproven that the patriarchal language of mainstream narrative film cannot be transformed and redeemed, that a woman's discourse cannot speak through it."[9] In deciding to position a nineteenth-century novel as the centerpiece of a study on feminist adaptation, with interpretation as the core objective to illustrate that a "woman's discourse [can] speak through it," I needed to incorporate fiction-into-film studies in my background preparation.

ADAPTATION AS CRITICISM

A substantial body of literature has accumulated on the methodology of comparing an original literary work and its adaptation as appropriate scholarly interpretation. As I reviewed this work, it became apparent why critics of so many persuasions are drawn to comparative studies. Such study widens the focus of inquiry and permits interesting speculative reasoning that illuminates both literature and cinema. Both arts, fiction and film, are preeminent in their respective centuries and have a historical interrelatedness, of which the treatment of women is a major, if long-ignored, correlation. Generally the focus of inquiry has centered on such questions as the ability of an adaptation to illuminate the original; issues of visual and narrative transformation, on inner thought and point of view, for example; the change that the passage of eras brings, particularly for social themes; and the intrinsic qualities of screenplay adaptations. Scholars are aided in this research today, regardless of area of focus, by the many published screenplays available for study. Quite a few screenplays are of adaptations never filmed, although they were written for proposed films. Such screenplays are now studied in their own right, as documents of interpretation, particularly those by noted writers, such as William Faulkner, Lillian Hellman, Harold Pinter, Malcolm Lowry, and Ruth Prawer Jhabvala.

Because the idea of adapting a novel as a critical methodology in itself is new, I relied for background on comparative analysis of traditional fiction-into-film criticism. This genre extends back to the landmark texts of film theory and represents a wide range of theoretical opinion.[10] For this study I am more interested in the attraction for and methodological issues of adaptation than in the disputes on differences between genres. Film scholar Marsha Kinder describes this perspective:

In dealing with a specific work of art, the critic can use a comparative method to define the particular combination of the unique and conventional elements, to understand the work's multiple functions for the individual and society, to evaluate how the artist has transformed the medium in order to express a particular vision. The deeper one moves into the individual work and the particular response to it, the more likely one is to break through to the general nature of the medium.[11]

For Dean Wilson Hartley adaptation is a catalytic agent through which difficult themes and passages become more accessible after the adapter locates equivalent cinematic tropes, descriptive metaphors, and subverbal themes, thereby "strengthen[ing] comprehension of the original work of art for the critical observer." Adaptation may "compress the material of a literary work without reducing its scope or damaging its uniqueness." In his study of adapter Kenneth Russell, Joseph A. Gomez extends this view: "The critic must analyze the properties unique to each [novel and film] so that finally a judgment is made about the nature of adaptation. What may take place then is an interweaving of art and ideas which spans the eras and reformulating in a form important in our own times, bridges the cultural gap of time by compression and enlargement." Gomez defines this as metaphase: "An attempt to evoke a certain feeling, and attitude and/or atmosphere which captures the character and the period."[12]

A significant contribution to fiction-into-film studies remains Regina Fadiman's 1978 study of the film based on Faulkner's novel *Intruder in the Dust*. Her book includes the screenplay and interpretive essays on the changing taste, attitudes, and aesthetic values in the United States during the period between the publication of Faulkner's novel and the film's release. Fadiman discusses the adaptation as a complex dialogue through which we see more of the original, "the polysemous nature of its origin and the centrifugal character of its implications." She affirms that to adapt is to select components that reveal the formal values of the novel and at the same time respond to the exigencies of a different medium, time period, and audience. Another adaptation study of a major American novel is the Morsebergers' essay on Truman Capote's scenario *The Innocents*, based on Henry James's *Turn of the Screw*. They read Capote's script as a critical analysis of James's novella when studied alongside the original: "An adaptation of a literary work to the screen can be seen as a critical interpretation of the work through another medium."[13]

Criticism of unfilmed screenplays is becoming more consequential in the literature. For example, Pinter's adaptation of Marcel Proust is frequently analyzed, as is Lowry's script for F. Scott Fitzgerald's *Tender Is the Night*. In an essay by Paul Tiessen and Miguel Mota, tribute is paid to Lowry's "homage" to Fitzgerald. The script contains as much "aesthetic integrity and legitimacy" as Fitzgerald's novel and is a work of art that may be read as a "de/re-construction" of the original. I noted with particular interest Tiessen and Mota's discussion of the screenplay's "marginalia"—comments within the primary text that elaborate on Fitzgerald, characters, music, and other connected material presented as a "running dialogue with the reader."[14]

In *Double Exposure: Fiction into Film*, Joy Gould Boyum recognizes that adaptation studies are caught between "conflicting aesthetic claims and rivalries" before she proceeds to make a cogent argument through case studies of the closeness of both sign systems and the relevance of adaptation studies. In a discussion of Pinter's Proust screenplay Boyum comments, "The finest adaptation is centered on the most sensitive reading of its source and it consequently exists not simply as art but as significant commentary."[15]

Noted critic Dudley Andrew argues persuasively for respect for the natural relationships between media and for fiction-into-film discourse. Describing adaptation as both a "leap and a process," Andrew remarks, "The hermeneutic circle, central to interpretation theory, preaches that an explication of a text occurs only after a prior understanding of it, yet that prior understanding is justified by the careful explication it allows." This "global conception" of a text means that the "explicit, foregrounded relation of a cinematic text to a well-constructed original text which it derives from and in some sense strives to reconstruct provides the analyst with a clear and useful laboratory condition." Further, "to probe the source of power" in the original by study of the ways both systems construct scenes and narratives which are commensurable is highly justifiable; Andrew maintains that "artistic adaptation poses no insurmountable obstacles."[16]

In his review of the history of adaptation theory Andrew concludes with a challenge to critics, "It's time for adaptation studies to take a sociological turn." In fact, this appears to be a direction in which adaptation studies are headed. In his study of German film Eric Rentschler proposes that critics "expand the field of adaptation study so as to include sociological, theoretical and historical dimensions, and to bring a livelier regard to the study of film and literature."[17]

In a thoughtful discussion of the film version of Brontë's *Jane Eyre* Jeffrey Sconce elucidates the idea of literature as being unstable over time: "A literary work is a history of its textual variants as well as the history of use and thought surrounding these texts as situated in a historical succession of cultural orders." Further, "Each time a new text, commentary or account of a work appears, including a film version, it constitutes both a reformation of the history of that work as well as a representation of the work newly formed within a specific, contemporary cultural moment." In this context I found Maureen Turim's phrase "semiotic layering" quite relevant. Turim describes her terminology as encompassing the "accrual and transformations of meanings associated with an artifact as it passes through history, or as it is presented in different versions." In another essay on Pinter's Proust screenplay, Mark Graham remarks on two aspects of screenplay study integral to this work. Because of the screenplay's intermediate position between novel and film it can "teach us about the language of film and that of literature and about their interrelationship." Then, "When the source and the adaptation are separated by time, the imprint of the latter's historical and cultural period is evident, and the original is necessarily recast in contemporary terms."[18]

In taking adaptation studies one step further by creating an original screenplay for interpretive purposes, I enter an area with almost no precedents. In fact, I found only one related study, Thomas Anderson's dissertation on Faulkner's *Light in August*, in which segments from the novel are adapted into both screenplay and chamber theater scenes. Anderson accompanies the scenes with critical judgments on similarities and diversities between the novel's prose and his transpositions. He explains how the novel's framework is probed, details the temporal and spatial locations of major structural components, and locates the action, scenes, and themes in time and space.

Anderson concludes, "If the adapter successfully creates visual analogues for the literary images, the adaptation may more faithfully
evoke the aesthetic impulses that were the novel than may the very
words of that novel when they are heard, rather than read by the
recipient." This methodology, as Anderson remarks, affirms the critical mode I propose: "A new work of art inspired by an existing work
[becomes in its own medium] a thematic and total analogy to the
original."[19] A perfect model awaited.

KATE CHOPIN AND "THE AWAKENING"

As I began to think about a case study of adaptation as feminist
interpretation, I made a mental catalogue of the many important
nineteenth-century women writers whose works only recently have
become available to literature scholars and students. The list includes
Mary Wilkins Freeman, Sarah Orne Jewett, Elizabeth Stoddard,
Frances Watkins Harper, and Elizabeth Stuart Phelps, as well as the
forgotten social protest work of better-known writers, such as Louisa
May Alcott. I knew that many of their novels, which I teach, would
make extraordinary films, given full liberty for the exposition of their
feminist motifs. But one novel in particular claimed my thoughts
and dreams.

I first read Kate Chopin's *The Awakening* in 1974 as part of an undertaking to study nineteenth-century women's fiction, and it has
never left me. I recall being struck by the beauty of the prose and the
relevance of the theme. Dwelling on Edna Pontellier's uncompromising search for autonomy, like other modern readers of the novel, I
asked how in 1899 did Chopin "know." Sometime later, in the midst
of an unrelated study of poetry, I recalled sentences from the novel,
evidently stored in memory, as lines from a poem. Returning to the
novel, I made the discovery that parts of it could be read as a long
poem in prose. Chopin, I knew, had claimed that her fiction came
from the "spontaneous expression of impressions gathered." How
then to explain the novel's precise structural design? I grew more

fascinated with Chopin's work and began to collect Chopin criticism, which was then much in evidence.

The Awakening is truly emblematic of the simultaneous movement in scholarship and society to seek a more balanced perspective on women's experience, culture, and status. In one of the first novels in the United States to treat the complexities of a woman's struggle to chart her own destiny, Chopin's heroine, Edna Pontellier, engages in self-discovery in the Louisiana of the eighteen-nineties. *The Awakening* is a very American novel, the work expressing a unique vitality in that the protagonist is a woman who projects a powerful and uncompromising individuality. Certainly Edna's quest, in the reverberations it has for our own time, gives the novel a charged reality for today's readers. By figuring Edna Pontellier as a rare portrayal of women's search for autonomy, I don't intend to imply that she represents all women. Although Edna is of the culture that Chopin knew best, the white ruling class, she doesn't even typify the women of that group, because she is so individualistic. Rather, she represents an idea. (Women of color and white working-class women are presences in the novel through their silence or their absence, points I will discuss in the interpretive chapter.)

Because of its advanced theme Chopin's novel suffered an unfortunate neglect when it was published in 1899. Rediscovered in the mid-twentieth century and later reappraised and critically acclaimed by feminist readers, the novel is at a peak of deserved interest. Chopin's own history as a woman artist in many ways parallels the theme and fate of her most famous work and is integral to the interpretation of her fiction.

In a recent study of the fiction of Edith Wharton and Kate Chopin, Mary Papke reflects on the obligations of studying women writers within historical and cultural contexts: "It is, of course, only a first step to place the work in its temporal reality; we obviously read the work from our time and its textual non-time, but we should also attempt to do justice to the writer's intent and critical expectations." Papke comments on critical advocacy to "enter the text" as part of the drive to comprehend "the elaboration of difference" in the literature of women's social protest novels.[20] I believe that aspects of Chopin's life and the social history of *The Awakening*'s reception bear on the relevance and timeliness of transforming this particular nine-teenth-century novel to a screenplay.

Kate Chopin brought four central attributes to her art: a conscious study of fiction and writing; an ability to observe human nature and behavior with uncanny insight; an "immense talent," as Chopin's character Adèle says to Edna about her painting; and an investigative fascination for women's status and destiny. To a remarkable extent, given the era and the milieu, Chopin's authorial voice resonates with universality and authenticity on the question of women's place in society. Chopin's theme makes her unique. Papke points out that Chopin's fiction (along with Edith Wharton's) is a "nonpolemical but political art in which the disruption of the rules of masculine/ feminine discourse and of the hegemonic world view is deeply but obviously embedded within character, plot, and theme." While Chopin critics stress that *The Awakening* is not autobiography, the critical realism of Edna is enmeshed with her creator. To "enter the text" one should become familiar with what is known about an author's life. Chopin has had three biographers. In the 1930s Daniel Rankin rescued Chopin's papers and interviewed people who knew her; in the 1960s Norwegian scholar Per Seyersted researched her life and work; and Emily Toth's important 1990 biography, the first full-length study of Chopin's life, reveals new information.[21] (For a comprehensive understanding of Chopin's life Toth's study should be consulted.)

A combination of the uniqueness of French society in America and fateful events that led to Chopin's growing up in a matriarchal household encouraged the streak of independence and absorption in women's status that mark her life and work. Born Katherine O'Flaherty in St. Louis in 1850 to an Irish-French family, Chopin experienced grief at an early age when her father, Thomas O'Flaherty, died in an accident. From that time on the five-year-old girl dwelled in a home with women in control: her mother, Eliza Faris O'Flaherty; her maternal grandmother, Athénaïs Charleville; and her maternal great-grandmother, Victoire Verdon Charleville. Chopin's mother had the "confident self-possession" of an aristocrat and considerable musical talent, but it was her great-grandmother who influenced the young girl's propensity toward independence and respect for women's struggles and accomplishments. She instilled in Chopin a "penetrating interest in character, particularly in independent women." Mme Charleville spent hours overseeing Chopin's daily music and French lessons and, more importantly for her future, telling Chopin intriguing stories about women's experiences. Those tales that derived from the Charleville family included reminiscences about Chopin's great-great-grandmother, Victoire Verdon, who when legally separated from her abusive husband operated a successful business, a line of keelboats shipping cargo between New Orleans and St. Louis. Chopin's female relatives, Daniel Rankin learned, had much pride in this matriarchal heritage.[22]

Kate Chopin's formal education at Sacred Heart Academy was uncompromisingly French and provincial, its mission to prepare girls to be Catholic wives and mothers. Yet the school was not without intellectual vigor. The curriculum, steeped in French culture, included classes in science, philosophy, literature, and current events, as well as religious studies. The girls were expected to be austerely pious and skilled in the domestic and social vocations. Male authority, in the guise of the Catholic church, determined the formal and informal daily program of the convent school. Chopin excelled as a student. The rigorous training suited her introspective nature.

The Civil War era brought much sadness into Chopin's life. During this period though, one anecdote, as told by Toth, exemplifies Chopin's character and spirit. A Union flag had been placed on the O'Flaherty porch, and risking arrest, she tore it down, an incident that made the adolescent girl famous in St. Louis.[23]

From Chopin's journal and Rankin's interviews, particularly with Sister Katherine Garesché, her school friend, a portrait emerges of a young woman who took her studies and music seriously and yearned for the reflective life. In *The Awakening* Edna reflects on the reserve of her own character and thinks of her childhood companion: "Her most intimate friend at school had been one of rather exceptional intellectual gifts, who wrote fine-sounding essays, which Edna admired and strove to imitate."[24] Reading was Chopin's favorite pastime. Her eclectic taste favored French and women writers, and included Maupassant, Daudet, de Staël, Charlotte Brontë, Austen, Susan Warner, and Margaret Oliphant.

Like Edna before she rebels, Chopin succumbed with seeming good grace to the social routine of the southern belle. But to her journal she confided her regret for time spent away from her true interests and her dislike for the vapid behavior of the young men custom expected young women to charm: "I dance with people I despise; amuse myself with men whose only talent lies in their feet."[25]

She remained at home until 1870, when at age twenty she married Oscar Chopin of Louisiana and moved with him to New Orleans, there beginning fifteen influential years. In Louisiana Chopin came to know the unique juxtaposition of liberal and repressive social codes set by the Creole patriarchy, in particular, severe cultural restraints somewhat held in check by the more liberal Spanish and Napoleonic legal codes, which gave white women the right to own and manage property inherited before marriage.[26] Little is known about the Chopin marriage, but the scant evidence indicates that the two shared a warm relationship. Kate Chopin exhibited unconventional tendencies for the time, such as walking about alone, which Oscar seemed to tolerate, although many thought her eccentric, and Oscar's provincial relatives expressed their chagrin. Oscar's sensitivity may relate to bitter memories of his father's cruel treatment of his own mother. The portrayal of Edna Pontellier's father is reminiscent of Kate Chopin's father-in-law: "The Colonel was perhaps unaware that he had coerced his own wife into her grave" (CW, 954). Between 1871 and 1879 Chopin gave birth to six children. Her inner feelings about motherhood, like those about her marriage, remain largely unknown. Nevertheless she is remembered as a devoted, loving mother, recalled warmly in interviews with adult Chopin children.

Oscar's cotton factoring business suffered setbacks, and the family moved to Natchitoches Parish in 1879, to the small village of Cloutier-ville, and began a new stage of family life. Oscar had inherited his father's plantation in the area and purchased additional land. Now he opened a general store and managed the property. Chopin made every effort to fit into village life and enjoyed a certain popularity balanced by disapproval of her behavior, which was considered even more eccentric in a rural area. Decades later local people recalled her oddities of dress and deportment, including horseback riding astride and alone, and smoking. They told Rankin she daringly let her ankle show when she stepped up on a curb.

Three years after the move to Cloutierville Oscar became ill and did not recover, dying from "swamp fever" in 1882. The tragedy plunged Chopin into active management of the store and property, for Oscar had left serious debts, and she needed to provide for six young children. She quickly developed the business acumen necessary to pay back debts and to keep the family going. It was her first taste of independence. Chopin used this episode of her life as background for the characterization of Thérèse Lafirme, the heroine of her first novel, *At Fault* (1890). Thérèse, a widow, is a very competent businesswoman and manager of her own plantation. Emily Toth tells an interesting anecdote from this period. Chopin had to petition the court to become the legal guardian of her children, because the law granted that right to the male parent. The court approved her request.[27]

In researching Chopin's life Toth broke through a wall of silence that had sheltered Chopin's secrets, shedding important new light on the author's understanding of romance and passion. In Cloutierville descendants of Chopin's peers told Toth about a scandal. Albert Sampite, a handsome planter, married, is linked to Chopin, although no actual record of their relationship exists except in recollections and disguised in fiction. Suddenly, two years after Oscar's death, Chopin moved back to St. Louis, and back to her mother's home. Toth points out that Chopin, in ending her romance to return to St. Louis, makes a choice similar to Edna's: "She chose herself."[28] Her fifteen years in Louisiana had been divided between the family home on Esplanade Street in the bustling French Quarter of New Orleans, summer idylls at Grand Isle, and the colorful region of Natchitoches Parish inhabited by Creoles, Cajuns, and former slaves.

In a life marred by the death of loved ones, grief came again, this time the truly devastating loss of Chopin's mother. For Chopin this period became a turning point. A close friend, Dr. Frederick Kolbenheyer, the model for the kindly Dr. Mandelet of *The Awakening*, had saved her Louisiana letters, a correspondence filled with artful description, and now he urged Chopin to turn to fiction, both to assuage her loneliness and to earn her livelihood. In time Chopin did begin to write, using the impressions of her Louisiana years for place and woman's emancipation for theme.

Chopin alludes to her "prior aimless existence" in a rare personal reference that relates to her rediscovery of Maupassant: "I was groping around; looking for something big, satisfying, convincing and finding nothing but—myself, a something neither big nor satisfying but wholly convincing." Elatedly she cites her reacquaintance with Maupassant: "Here was life, not fiction."[29] This discovery, along with her friend's encouragement, her economic need, and probably the release of long-repressed ambition, became the starting point of her writing career. When her first published story, "A Point at Issue," which is about a woman activist, appeared in 1889, Chopin was thirty-nine years old.

It will probably never be known if she actually did experience the pull of ambition and independence beyond the roles of wife and mother before this belated professional achievement, but there are intriguing hints that she did. Per Seyersted suggests that Chopin conducted a long dialogue with herself on the conflict of roles as she experienced her artistic development. Years later, her career and reputation well established, Chopin confided to her diary: "If it were possible for my husband and mother to come back to earth, I feel that I would unhesitatingly give up everything that has come into my life since they left it and join my existence again with theirs. To do that, I would have to forget the past ten years of my growth—my real growth."[30] In an 1894 published interview, her poet friend William Schuyler suggests the idea of thwarted ambition: "Perhaps had Mrs. Chopin's environment been different, her genius might have developed twenty years sooner than it did." In the introduction to Chopin's collected works Seyersted notes that she felt marriage and motherhood lacked sufficient purpose and that her literary career may be interpreted developmentally in "the increasing self-confidence and daring of her heroines."[31]

Chopin's tendency to rebel against established rules guiding women's behavior is much a part of her history, and she seems to have understood her behavior as small acts of defiance against repressive traditions. As early as her honeymoon trip, she walked about in solitude and confided in her journal, "I wonder what people thought of me—a young woman strolling about alone."[32]

She enjoyed success as a writer because of her consummate skill and the exotic Louisiana culture and setting portrayed in her stories. Regional writing was popular during the 1890s and there was a ready audience, particularly in the East, for Chopin's tales. Yet, even with the publication of the early stories in distinguished periodicals such as *Century, Vogue,* and *Atlantic Monthly,* some of her fictional themes about women's rebellion and sensuality were too unconventional for the literary establishment. Chopin either toned down the objectionable parts or resubmitted the stories to more liberal publications.[33]

During those years in St. Louis Chopin had opportunities to remarry, but she chose to remain single. Photographs attest to her beauty and sophisticated demeanor, while the recollections of friends and family accumulate details about her intelligence, charm, and wit. She belonged to a circle of progressive St. Louis intellectuals, professionals, and artists and held a favored position as a popular hostess. Chopin kept occupied with her writing and associated details, particularly financial records; family and friends; visits to Louisiana and travels East on literary business; and always, the solitary pursuits that she savored.

Any inspiration for the theme of women's inequality that Chopin found in her own life was buttressed by the situation of anonymous women in her milieu. The journals, letters, and memoirs of the era supply ample evidence of repressed lives, passive acceptance, and intellectual and emotional rebellion. In a memoir of the era, Caroline Merrick recalls the time when she and a cousin are told by her father to dismount their horses because it is improper for two young ladies to be seen on a public road so early in the morning: "I early ascertained that girls had a sphere wherein they were expected to remain and the despotic hand of some man was continually lifted to keep them revolving in a certain prescribed and restricted orbit."[34]

During Chopin's era, feminist thought and activism became a concern.[35] The standard for Victorian women emphasized obligation to the patriarchal code, and this dependency explains the adaptive nature of a philosophy of feminism that looked for reform within the traditional institutions while stressing the moral superiority of women. Chopin, with her more advanced outlook and European focus, believed that women and men had similar drives and deserved the same rights. In her fiction Chopin developed women characters who tried to be honest about their own needs and instincts. The central character is typically a woman in conflict with culturally prescribed roles who strives to obtain a unique solution.

In nearly ninety short stories, many gathered in the collections *Bayou Folk* (1894) and *A Night in Acadie* (1897), Chopin returns again and again to the theme of women's emancipation. Her tone varies.

She is snide to the self-effacing Mrs. Benoite, who "show[ed] a certain lack of self assertion which her husband regarded as the perfection of womanliness" ("The Gentleman from New Orleans," *CW,* 631). She approves of the independent Pauline in "A Mental Suggestion": Pauline's "mental poise was a rebuke to [Faverham]; there was a constant rebuff in her lack of the coquettish, the captivating, the feminine" (*CW,* 548). The theme of women's independence is unusually powerful in "The Story of an Hour," in which a woman learns of her husband's death and exclaims to herself: "Free! Body and soul free!" (*CW,* 354). When she discovers the report of his death is false, she falls dead from, it is implied, the shock of the disappointment. In 1894 this theme was too unorthodox, and the story was refused publication several times before *Vogue* accepted it. Chopin continued to write her short stories and also published a novel, *At Fault* (1889).[36]

In 1897 Chopin began work on a new novel. The protagonist, like Chopin, is a woman of the South; she knows marriage and motherhood, cultivates her artistic talent, and thrusts herself into rebellion in quest of autonomy. Moreover, her search for fulfillment includes attending to the desires of her sensual nature. This theme proved costly to Chopin's career and well-being.

When the avant-garde firm of Herbert S. Stone and Company of Chicago published *The Awakening* in 1899, several favorable reviews, although by interested parties, must have reassured Chopin. Then the critical reception, for which the book is known, quickly gained ascendancy, setting the stage for one of the most interesting episodes in U.S. literary critical history. Nearly all Chopin scholars refer, either briefly or in detail, to the abusive criticism *The Awakening* received, a history that in some ways parallels injustices defined in the novel.

Most reviewers labeled the novel "scandalous" and found its theme morbid and untrue, calling it "hideous," "poison[ous]," "indelicate," "loathsome," "vulgar," or "unhealth[ily] introspective."[37] Overeager to discredit the novel's theme while guardedly praising its literary qualities, critics misrepresented the novel, adding exaggeration to hostility by claiming, for example, "detailed and *manifold* [emphasis added] love affairs of a wife and mother."[38]

The tendency to misread the novel and to disregard the more subtle nuances of characterization suggest that Kate Chopin struck a moral chord that even today has the power to disturb deeply em-

bedded ideas of sexual roles. Rebellious themes still draw out submerged resistance to women's equality. The outrage focused on
Chopin's assertions that a married woman has sexual feelings and
may not be totally selfless, a problem exacerbated because Edna Pontellier's transgression went unrepented and unpunished. Victorian
America could not tolerate the portrayal of a woman who defied and
escaped the narrow confines of her role. While it is not known exactly how many copies were sold, Chopin's records indicate that she
earned $102 in royalties the first year of publication, and very little
thereafter.[39]

Taken aback by the ridicule and rejection that followed the novel's
publication, Chopin in self-defense and as a carefully disguised re-
buttal published her own review, which reads in part: "Having a
group of people at my disposal, I thought it might be entertaining
(to myself) to throw them together and see what would happen. I
never dreamed of Mrs. Pontellier making such a mess of things, and
working out her own damnation as she did."[40] Needless to say,
Chopin did take her protagonist seriously. Chopin's daughter, Lelia
Hattersley, told Rankin that her mother never spoke of her disappointment. Afterwards, Chopin wrote only several stories for children and one remarkable long story, "Charlie," in which, for the
first time, she expresses an overt psychological anger toward men. In
this story of female independence, Charlie's (Charlotte's) father has
an accident that necessitates the amputation of his arm. The roles
reverse between father and daughter as Charlie takes care of him
and also learns to manage his business affairs. Chopin's hurt is also
shown in a fragment titled "Reflections," in which she depicts herself as "weeping" alongside the "moving procession that has left
[her] by the road-side!" (CW, 622) "Stunned and bewildered" by the
unexpected collapse of her literary career, Chopin never recovered
her drive and lapsed into indifference, like many other women artists who lack an appreciative audience. She had worked in isolation,
removed from a community of like-minded associates; consequently,
she lacked the kind of support that can offset rejection with understanding and comfort.

Chopin achieved success as a writer of short stories. After *The
Awakening* she more than likely intended to continue to explore the
more complex form of the novel. This is perhaps the most poignant

speculation that attends her life. She lived quietly for several more years and died in 1904 after suffering a brain hemorrhage at the St. Louis World's Fair.

Through the first fifty years of the twentieth century *The Awakening* remained obscure. The few literary histories that mention Chopin's Louisiana tales do not discuss her masterpiece. The one exception of the era is Rankin's biography, in which he views the novel as an unfortunate departure for the "Louisiana regionalist." In the 1940s, Cyrille Arnavon, a professor of French, found a copy of *The Awakening* in a Paris bookshop and published a French translation in 1953 with an enthusiastic introduction.[41] This fortunate rediscovery led to *The Awakening*'s reevaluation as a major work of U.S. fiction. Arnavon's student at Harvard, Per Seyersted, took up the study of Chopin and became instrumental in the recovery of Chopin's literary reputation. By 1969 he had published a study of her life and work and had edited two volumes of her fiction and nonfiction. Seyersted saw Chopin as a precursor of psychological realism and the existential dilemma, "a rare, transitional figure in modern literature." She broke new ground and had the qualities of vision and originality to "give us [a] great novel," defying "tradition with a daring which we can hardly fathom today." Seyersted concludes, she "undertook to give the unsparing truth about woman's submerged life. She was something of a pioneer in the treatment of amoral sexuality, of divorce, and of woman's urge for an existential authenticity."[42]

Following Seyersted, the initial era of critical reevaluation emphasized *The Awakening*'s advanced style, remarking on the way the work anticipates such twentieth-century writers as Joyce and D. H. Lawrence.[43] Out of print for more than half a century, the novel, first reissued in a paperback edition in 1964, is now available in many editions. The critical ambivalence that greeted the novel in 1899— praise for its art, condemnation for its themes—attests to the severe misogyny that controlled the restricted lives women led. Now the concurrent emphasis on women's status in society and the recognition of women's art have enabled *The Awakening* to reach the wide audience and acclaim Chopin's novel merits. The modern appraisal of *The Awakening*, set in motion by Arnavon, enlarged upon by Seyersted, and buttressed by influential critics, entered a new and exciting phase of criticism in the early 1970s that has not abated. The feminist critical reappraisal of Chopin's novel set out to "see with fresh eyes," as Adrienne Rich's often quoted decree challenges, thereby gradually revealing its profound, complex, and remarkable meanings. At the same time, aspects of the novel's mysterious sensibilities continue to resist interpretation.

At the heart of the furor the novel unleashed is its rebellious theme: a woman's search for authenticity. The theme of self-identity comprises a major focal point of contemporary feminist criticism. By virtue of its absolute commitment to self-fulfillment the novel stands alone. As Joyce Ladenson points out, "It is startling to read *The Awakening* with the awareness that it was written in the absence of today's feminist consciousness, for, in many significant ways, the novel is a foreshadowing of the kind of female *bildungsroman* which characterizes the works of [contemporary women writers]."[44]

The novel has proven to be a source for many of the discoveries of feminist literary criticism. Because my study has a historical focus and my adaptation seeks to incorporate the novel's fate through time, I sought out representative ideas from the several eras of criticism to interweave with my own ideas about the novel to enrich the screenplay's meaning and value. For example, an influential essay by Annette Kolodny, published in 1975, still appears fresh in its critical approach. Kolodny defines three characteristics that she locates in women's writing: inversion, reflexive perception, and the fear of inauthenticity. Kolodny is one of the first critics to note that in *The Awakening,* as in many contemporary women's novels, "love is revealed as violence and romance as fraud; suicide and death are imaged as comforting and attractive, while loneliness and isolation become, for their heroines, means to self-knowledge and contentment."[45]

At the same time, Eliane Jasenas wrote about the French influence in *The Awakening.* Jasenas discusses French authors Chopin knew well, particularly Maupassant, whose stories Chopin translated. Jasenas notes that Chopin rejects Maupassant's portrait of womanhood "as the best expression of animalism in man": "Chopin transformed Maupassant's general pessimism and his special antagonism toward women into a set of conditions upon which Edna would have to retrieve herself." As Edna progresses toward self-discovery she never experiences self-revulsion as Maupassant's heroines do. Jasenas suggests that Edna's search "is the beauty of a destiny in which emancipation and self-awareness take the quality of a heroic task leading towards spiritual accomplishment."[46]

While the incisive analyses of such 1980s critics as Cynthia Griffin Wolff and Sandra M. Gilbert illuminate Chopin's novel, the 1990s I believe have ushered in a more theoretical period in Chopin criticism. Emblematic of this analysis is Jean Wyatt's chapter on Chopin in her study *Reconstructing Desire*. Wyatt calls *The Awakening* a "doubly revolutionary" work that through its semiotic language and "its intrusions of physical experience break[s] down the unified self-concept of the reader by appealing to a dimension usually repressed from realistic texts: the body," and that exposes "a reader's heterogeneity without going beyond the personal and subjective." In an essay on "Gendered Doubleness" Marianne DeKoven places Chopin's novel, historically categorized as a realist text, in the modernist canon. She cites its decentered subjectivity, rupture of linearity in plot and temporal structure, presymbolic language, and stylistic indeterminacy, and the "shock" of violation of expected continuities. As a female modernist text, *The Awakening*, DeKoven argues, reflects Chopin's ambivalence between seeking freedom and autonomy and fearing the "potential for bringing on retribution from a still-empowered patriarchy."[47]

Underlying and even unifying fiction-into-film criticism is the desire to "see" more deeply. This need provides a primary connection between art, interpretation, and audience. In an essay praising Maupassant, a writer she much admired, Kate Chopin through her enthusiasm conveys her own affinity to this ideal: "Here was a man who had escaped from tradition and authority, who had entered into himself and looked out upon life through his own being and with his own eyes; and who, in a direct and simple way, told us what he *saw*" (*CW*, 701; emphasis added). Chopin told what she had seen, and through my adaptation of her witnessing I seek to tell what I have seen. (In a most interesting way Kate Chopin's fiction anticipates film and lends itself to cinematic adaptation.[48] This became clear as I studied *The Awakening* alongside the adaptation literature, as I will explain in the interpretive chapter.)

The idea to combine several compelling interests in one study became irresistible: first, to test creative impulses without risking too great a leap into uncharted areas; then, to immerse myself in the novel to attempt to unmask the "beloved text"; finally, to formulate in a form appropriate for our own time a significant precursor with its strengths intact and its relevance reemphasized. I hope to illustrate that the rare theme of an uncompromising quest for female autonomy may be transposed with its complex portrayal intact. The process encompasses an effort to fuse timeliness of theme with timeliness of form, thereby making the novel even more accessible. This experimental analysis of *The Awakening* constitutes both rediscovery and invention. Because for Kate Chopin womanhood itself was a state yet to be discovered, a quest that is still a focus of feminist struggle, the transformation of Chopin's novel into a screenplay is appropriate at this time. The methodology of adaptation as criticism should take interpretation of Chopin's novel deeper into the realm of female/male polarities and contribute to the current theoretical and pragmatic discourse, capsuled by Haskell's phrase, to "reinvent the feminine self" through the search for an unfettered female authenticity. Or as Chopin put it, "She [Edna] was seeking herself and finding herself" (*CW*, 934).

PREPARING TO BE AN ADAPTER

As background for the adaptation I began with Kate Chopin and read all of her fiction, nonfiction, biographical studies, and criticism, from early book reviews to contemporary studies, especially feminist criticism. I read Chopin's contemporaries, including Grace King and Lafcadio Hearn, and nineteenth-century documents, including women's diaries, newspapers, and magazines, as well as social histories of the times, to understand family relationships, sanctioned activities, the ennui of daily life, apparel style, and related customs. I reviewed the decorative arts of Louisiana, local architecture, the musical taste of the times, and U.S. impressionism, and I spent time in New Orleans.

I studied film theory, particularly adaptation criticism and feminist film theory, and viewed as many films as possible, both adaptations (often available to late-night television habitués) and contemporary films, especially those that evoked a mood or style related to my interests in *The Awakening* adaptation.

I studied screenplay writing. I read many screenplays, particularly the classics in the field such as Alain Robbe-Grillet's screenplay for *Last Year at Marienbad* (1962). At first glance a nineteenth-century novel set in southern Louisiana and Robbe-Grillet's ultramodern text have little in common. Yet the very modernity of his screenplay lends credence to the objective of transforming Chopin's work to a contemporary form. The scenario is deliberately literary, incorporating camera instructions into the narrative and presenting the theme in a suggestive, even labyrinthine tone.

I practiced screenplay writing. I recalled reading how screenwriter Edward Anhalt begins the adaptation process by tearing from the novel pages that interest him and arranging them in various sequences until the filmic reconstruction makes itself clear. One day I found myself with two identical paperback copies of *The Awakening* in front of me, scissors at hand. I systematically cut the books into units of scenes, paragraphs, and even sentences. I taped these sections to large index cards and annotated, arranged, and rearranged them for days afterward, an exercise that took me deeper into the work. Although I abandoned this process when I became ready to begin the screenplay, this almost surgical procedure led me into the intricacies of interpretation through adaptation.

"THE AWAKENING": PLOT SUMMARY

I have chosen not to include scenes from *The Awakening* to compare with the screenplay because so many editions of the novel are readily available in paperback. More importantly, I hope that readers of the screenplay who have not read Chopin's novel will be induced to do so. I offer a plot summary with the caution that the simplicity of the plot does little justice to the richness of the novel.

The story opens at Grand Isle, Louisiana, a summer resort on the Gulf for wealthy New Orleans Creole families. The era is the early 1890s. Edna Pontellier, a young married woman with two small sons, finds herself vaguely discontented. Over the summer she begins to question her existence. The other characters—her friends Adèle Ratignolle and Mademoiselle Reisz; Robert Lebrun, the son of the proprietor; children; and on weekends, husbands, including her own, Léonce—all play a role in Edna's "awakenings." A series of events that may seem rather insignificant—quarreling with her husband, learning how to swim, developing a romantic interest, and engaging in contemplative thought about her past and future—propel her toward the realization that she is entrapped by social conventions. Back in the city, as fall arrives, Edna takes more overt and dramatically unconventional actions to advance her sense of autonomy. Her sons are sent to their grandmother in the country. She goes against her husband's wishes. She once again takes up her interest in painting. She takes long walks unescorted. She refuses to stay home for the traditional reception-day callers. She moves out of the family home into a small cottage she can call her own. And she has a brief affair that awakens her sensual nature, although she is not in love. Edna weighs her responsibilities as a wife and a mother against her ability to live her life without compromise. She returns alone to Grand Isle, sheds her clothing by the shore, and swims out until she grows tired. There the novel ends.

EDNA

A Screenplay of *The Awakening*

ACT I

Time: 1891–92
Locale: New Orleans and Grand Isle, Louisiana

**Scene 1. Future time, prologue: Spring. A death announcement
is delivered to Dr. Mandelet.**

The opening shot shows a slow fade on the closely bedded spring
flowers of a southern cottage garden. Bougainvillea trail through the
carved rails of a low ironwork fence, and an untamed hibiscus suggests the tropical. The colors are vibrant, the shapes indistinct; the
shadowless sunlight weighs heavily, as a silence. The moment lingers; then the air of expectancy is realized by a shot of JOE's hand as
he unlatches the gate.

Joe is the young black houseboy of the Pontelliers. He is dressed
in somber livery and carries a large silver basket. A series of oddly
angled shots accompany his movements: his lower legs on the bricked
path; a startled bird (the whir of wings); his upper body; the basket;
the Dutch door of the cottage office, bottom-half closed, top-half
latched outward; and the sign, "Dr. Mandelet."

Large on the screen is the oversized card Joe hands over the door-
sill; on it is the silhouette of a weeping willow, bordered with a wide
black strip.

The camera pulls back to reveal an English study in which the
furniture, books, and objects are all carelessly arranged. DR. MAN-
DELET, who is rather hefty, rises, though only his side and arm are
visible, to take the card. Joe's retreating steps resound on the path.
The doctor sinks back in his desk chair.

From over his shoulder we see him raise the card until it fills the frame. As he opens and lowers the card, the view that it had obscured—the garden, seen from an open window—fills the screen. Now there is only the garden through the window. The sun shimmers, and tall gladiola gently sway. Offscreen a solitary bird chirps.

Scene 2. Present time: Spring. Edna comforts Adèle.

A dissolve to rippling water fills the screen. A woman's face is dimly reflected in its gentle motion. A sudden splash disturbs the image, and then the strong, shapely hands of EDNA PONTELLIER wring a white cloth. The camera moves back just enough to disclose the rippling water in a basin on a dry sink. Edna's bending figure straightens up. She sprinkles the cloth with cologne. Scattered on the pale marble counter are several cologne bottles, a brush-and-comb set, and a pair of jet earrings.

From a low tilt across a white coverlet, the camera focuses on the turning figure of Edna. She is in her late twenties, tall, with an aristocratic demeanor. Her features are unremarkable; yet when considered as a whole, they comprise a beauty that is arresting. The collar of her beige gown is open, and the lavender belt is loosely wrapped. It is warm in the room. Edna lightly kneads her neck.

Now a low hum of a haunting melody is heard [Kay Gardner, "Mooncircles"]. The camera turns to the head of the bed and stops on ADÈLE RATIGNOLLE, who is restlessly posed there. Adèle's romantic beauty is dimmed by the onset of labor. Her thick blond hair is coiled on the pillow. The camera pulls back and up as Edna places the cooling cloth on her friend's brow. As Adèle slides the fingers of one hand over the coverlet, she looks up at Edna, who brings her arm to rest on the ornately carved headboard. Edna slowly turns her head and gazes into the camera.

Scene 3. Reverie: Summer. The sewing lesson.

The Lebrun Hotel on Grand Isle includes a main house and twelve frame cottages. A covered gallery connecting the buildings is, like the small cottage porches, painted white. It has an unadorned rail. This morning, Adèle, who is large in the frame, walks along the gallery. She carries a sewing basket in front of her. The humming stops. This continuing shot of Adèle is interposed with a series of small vignettes depicting the day's activities. VICTOR LEBRUN, who is nineteen, rolls a carriage wheel down the parkway; small children in cumbersome costumes play croquet under the water oaks that line the far border of the long sloping lawn; and a black child delivers mail to the cottages. Also, an elderly WIDOW, one of the guests, who is dressed in black and has a pious air, reads on her porch. Adèle nods to her as she passes by. Adèle reaches the Pontellier cottage and calls through the screen door:

ADÈLE: Chérie, let's sit on the porch. There's a little breeze.
EDNA: (Offscreen) A moment, Adèle.

Adèle unfolds a paper pattern and cloth on an oblong wicker table. She is already pinning the pattern when Edna walks into the frame. The camera moves back to a position that bisects the screen with the porch rail. Edna settles herself in the rocker, at an angle to the rail, and places her book and candy box on the floor. Behind her, a parasol leans against the wall.

EDNA: How can you think of winter pajamas on such a day?

Adèle, intent on her task, reaches for the scissors.

EDNA: I wonder where Robert went?
ADÈLE: Now for Raoul this should be one size larger. So, let's cut two inches past the edge. Do you agree?

Edna looks out over the lawn.

EDNA: He promised to read to us. (Pause) It's the last chapter.
ADÈLE: (As she cuts) Alphonse is very concerned. Each year the influenza grows worse.
EDNA: Léonce's mother suggested our boys come to her.

During this dialogue Edna reaches for the parasol. She absent-mindedly opens and closes it.

EDNA: She would like nothing better.

Adèle unpins the pattern and it falls to the floor.

ADÈLE: I couldn't bear to be parted from my precious little ones.

The camera draws closer to Edna as she places the open book in her lap.

EDNA: Not even for their own good?

The image changes to a shot from over Adèle's shoulder to Edna. Edna looks up at her friend.

ADÈLE: Of course. My children are my very life.

The camera returns to the in-front-of-the-porch position, but at a different angle than the earlier shot. Adèle wipes her face with a large lacy handkerchief.

ADÈLE: Here, Edna. (She picks up the pattern.) It's not at all difficult.

Adèle decides to rest; she sits down in a small chair next to the table.

ADÈLE: What are you reading?
EDNA: (She looks into the air.) "There was the hum of bees, and the musky odor of pinks filled the air." [Gardner, "Pisces"]

Edna opens the candy box and extends it to Adèle.

ADÈLE: (With a wave of her hand) Too rich. (She looks into the box.) Perhaps a cream. (She tastes it.) Alphonse is so particular about my diet now.
EDNA: (With a merry laugh) A Creole baby is born with a taste for praline.
ADÈLE: (Somberly) One can't be too careful.
EDNA: Must everything be a sacrifice?
ADÈLE: Whatever do you mean, Chérie?
EDNA: I'm only beginning to understand it myself. (Pause) Try a chocolate, Adèle?
ADÈLE: (She rises.) Now we will cut Etienne's.

Scene 4. Present time: Spring. Edna and Adèle, the waiting.

Adèle's bedroom is viewed as a stage set. The camera is stationary. A suite of eighteenth-century French country furniture fills the bedroom. Spanish religious icons are prominently displayed. Statues of the saints are set in wall niches. It is dusk; the gas lamps give a soft light. Several figures, barely realized, move about the room. Their elongated shadows are reflected on the wall. Adèle lies on the lounge at the foot of the bed. Then she half sits up, with her head supported by many pillows. Edna sits beside her on a small stool. She holds a stereoscope in her lap. A NURSE kneels by the fireplace. This woman, who is black, is dressed traditionally, with a tall *tignon* (wrapped scarf) on her head. She rises and comes to Adèle's side with a medicine bottle.

ADÈLE: When will the doctor arrive? What time is it?

The camera moves close to the hem of Edna's gown. A view-card of the American West has fallen to the carpet. Edna bends down to retrieve the card.

Scene 5. Reverie: Summer. Edna and Robert,
The swimming lesson.

The field of the image is the spacious porch of the Lebrun Hotel main house, centering on the French doors of the entrance. Pale green wicker furniture is arranged in formal groupings. Two wicker bird cages hang at each side of the wide doorway. A white crested cockatiel swings in one, and in the other a parrot breaks the silence with an intermittent call. A large Mexican pot is placed to the side, between the door and the broad porch steps. ROBERT LEBRUN, in a white suit, steps out onto the porch. He pauses and lights a cigarette. Robert is a blond good-looking young man, yet he seems ordinary. Both he and the viewer gaze along the porch across to the gallery.

With a quick cut, the camera shoots over Robert's shoulder and locates the retreating figure of Edna. Robert hurries forward, his left side large in the frame. The image changes: Edna and Robert walk together along the gallery as the camera tracks ahead of them.

ROBERT: Are you going down to the beach?

EDNA: Oh no. I think not. Perhaps I'll work on Adèle's portrait.

ROBERT: At breakfast Madame Ratignolle said she was not at all well.

EDNA: But she looks ravishing today!

ROBERT: You mustn't miss your lesson. (Pause) The water is so inviting this time of day.

They reach the Pontellier porch. The camera moves in close as Robert takes Edna's large straw hat from its wall peg. Then, with only his arms visible in a curving border of the screen, he places it gently on her head.

ROBERT: (offscreen) Come, it will do you good.

Edna, alone in the frame, straightens her hat in a gesture identical to Robert's. She stares out over the lawn. From Edna's perspective we follow her gaze [Ernest Guiraud, "Sylvia"]. The lawn is similar to a large meadow; it is slightly inclined and well mowed. It ends where a stand of huge ancient water oaks line the wooded area beyond. The lush growth of trees, vines, and shrubs in the background becomes more visible as the camera pans down the lawn. Overgrown citrus trees are all that remain of the former grove. The camera hits upon a break in the foliage and stops abruptly where a path begins.

In the middle distance, off to the side, the camera tracks Edna and Robert as they stroll down the lawn. The two pause; Robert dashes back to the porch where he retrieves Edna's parasol. He hurries back and opens the pink-lined sunshade for her.

A new shot catches the top of Edna's and Robert's bent heads (the parasol is tilted back) as they walk along the path to the beach. This is a narrow, twisting, sandy trail, bordered by tall plants, orange trees, and clumps of yellow flowers. Runners reach across the ground as though intent on closing this gap in the dense woods. The image shifts to a series of shots, low to the ground, that mark Edna's and Robert's progress. The camera at times stays just ahead: it catches a foot as it moves into the frame, then a glimpse of Edna's gown brushing the ground; the waxy yellow flowers appear in closeup, and grains of sand are blown by their steps. Robert's leg is angled as it moves into the frame; Edna's hand is in closeup as she brushes a branch aside; and all the while there is the low murmur of voices and the occasional sound of a twig snapping underfoot. These shots are interposed with views of the glistening deep green branches overhead, heavy with unripe fruit. The final images are a turn in the path, then, suddenly, open beach as Edna and Robert reach the Gulf shore.

A close shot: Edna's face, at ease, open. From her perspective we follow the view along the wide stretch of sand and out to the sea. It is a beautiful scene, still and rather deserted. In the middle distance one or two sails bob slowly. The sea is smooth at half-tide, and low green ripples break on the shore. A YOUNG COUPLE, obviously infatuated with each other, sit on two beach chairs close to the water's edge. Meanwhile, Victor swims earnestly back and forth.

Reverse angle: from the shoreline to the colorful row of bathhouses set against the wooded background. From the porch of one of the bathhouses, an elderly guest, MONSIEUR FARIVAL, reads his newspaper.

The camera cuts to the porch of another one of the bathhouses, then to its door. Reverse angle: from within the dark interior Edna's hand pushes the door open. Another cut to the porch front as she emerges in her bathing costume. Edna looks seaward. The camera cuts to Robert as he waves from the shallows. The camera turns to Edna, who appears not to notice him.

The image changes: small waves spill on the beach and rapidly recede. The subtle sounds of the sea become more distinct. The sun casts a sparkling light over this enticing image of sea and shore.

A new shot: Edna and Robert stand alongside each other but apart as they walk into the sea. When they reach waist-deep water, they pause and smile at each other (this is the first time Edna smiles). The camera moves back to the middle distance. Edna takes Robert's hand and lowers herself in the water to splash playfully like a child. In a moment she straightens up and looks longingly to the right. The image shifts to Victor, as he dives from a small anchored wooden raft. The sound of children's voices is heard, and the camera turns toward shore. Several boys and girls race toward the sea and then wheel about as their nurse calls to them.

The camera returns to Edna and Robert as they stand face-to-face in the water. The sea gently laps at their waists.

ROBERT: Are you ready for your lesson, Mrs. Pontellier?

The camera pulls back as Edna looks toward Victor, who now swims toward shore. The camera follows him as Edna speaks off-screen.

EDNA: Is it so foolish of me?

Scene 6. Present time: Spring. Adèle's children say goodnight.

This next shot is very formal. As before, the camera shoots into Adèle's bedroom as though it were a stage set. Adèle half reclines on the lounge, and Edna sits at the foot of the bed, with her back against the tall post. The three little nightgowned RATIGNOLLE CHILDREN line up alongside the lounge. Adèle clasps the hand of the littlest one and pulls her toward her. In the doorway is the dim figure of ALPHONSE RATIGNOLLE. He is tall, thin, and has a tapered moustache.

ALPHONSE: I hear the doctor's coach.

Scene 7. Past time: Summer. Edna and Léonce quarrel.

It is evening, and the small bedroom of the Pontellier summer cottage is rather dark. The camera makes a slow circular movement around the pleasingly crowded room and surveys the dim shapes of an armoire and a liquor cabinet, and the disarray of clothes. White lace curtains hang at the window and porch door. The camera stops at the dresser mirror, which reflects a canopied bed. Edna is asleep on her side, an arm across her face. The camera turns to the inner door, which is draped with a beaded curtain.

LÉONCE PONTELLIER enters the room. He is in his thirties, of average height and dark complexion. In close shot Léonce lights the dresser lamp and looks over at the bed. The camera moves back so that both Léonce at the dresser, and Edna in bed, are visible in the frame. He appears to be in high spirits as he empties his pockets. Léonce takes out a roll of money and counts it. Then he turns and holds it up to Edna. Léonce shrugs as he puts it down. He will pick up the money one more time, toss it in his hand and set it down with a smile. Edna sighs sleepily and changes position in accompaniment with his chatter.

LÉONCE: What cards I held tonight! I tell you, Edna, I couldn't lose. (Pause) Old Krantz was celebrating. It was brandy on the house— the very finest, too! The Lebruns could take a lesson. (Pause) It's time they thought about improvements. Krantz is bringing in an old street railway to carry guests from the hotel to the beach. How's that for an idea?

Léonce looks at Edna with annoyance; then he stalks out of the room. The camera follows his retreating figure down the dark inner hall and into the room where the Pontellier sons, RAOUL, who is five, and ETIENNE, who is four, are sleeping. The camera moves in close. Only Léonce's arms are seen as he adjusts the boys' covers. One of the children sleepily mutters a phrase from his dream that sounds like, "fishing cap."

Léonce's arm is still large on the screen, only now he bends over Edna, touching her lightly and saying softly:

LÉONCE: Edna, Raoul is feverish. Edna?

The image changes. Léonce stands in front of the liquor cabinet while he lights a cigar. Edna is propped up on her arms in bed. With her eyes she follows Léonce as he walks over to the window.

LÉONCE: (He gestures with the hand that holds the cigar.) Ah, it's all in my hands. Our son needs you. (He walks to the inner door.) Can I be expected to—

In the midst of this monologue Edna springs up with a harassed air and rushes out of the room. Léonce's words fade away. Then we see Edna as she bends over the sleeping children and gently brushes Raoul's forehead. It is quiet. Edna remains in the shadowy room for a moment, as though to compose herself. The camera shifts to a toy clock on the dresser. Then the image returns to the Pontellier's bedroom. Edna sits wearily on the edge of the bed, and Léonce changes into nightclothes.

LÉONCE: Didn't I tell you? How is he? (Pause) Too much sun, I . . .

Ah, that stupid Mulâtresse. She'll have a surprise in the morning. I've been far too lenient.

He extinguishes the lamp. Edna is still visible in the shadows, poised on the edge of the bed. From across the bed comes Léonce's voice.

LÉONCE: Edna, when I'm in the city, you must look after things. Come to bed. (Placatingly) You will tire yourself.

During the speech the camera moves closer to Edna [Frédéric Chopin, Sonata No. 2 in B-Flat Minor, Op. 35]. Her cheeks are wet. Now the image changes: Edna is at the porch door; she parts the curtains. The view from the porch doorway is barely visible; the dark contours are softened by a lamp or two somewhere on the property. For a brief second the starry sky comes unnaturally close. Then there is a partial view of Edna with her fingertips pressed against the screen door.

A new shot: Edna sits stiffly in the porch rocker in the foreground of the screen, but she is only partially in view. Vague landscape shadows are seen, and the edge of a building. Uncertain night sounds are heard—an owl calls from his perch, and a dog answers with a growl. In the mild breeze branches move slightly. There is the murmur of the sea.

Reverse angle: the camera frames the rocker from the right. Edna leans back; her tears fall freely, but silently. With an edge of her wide sleeve she wipes them away. The camera moves closer, and insects buzz; Edna waves an arm about her face. Then from her perspective, but telescoped closer, we see the water oaks with their twisting limbs. The draped Spanish moss looks mysterious in the dark. The image changes to a shot where the path begins, the camera low to the ground. This is held for a moment, and then there is a cut to Edna who stands in the porch doorway and looks out; her figure is half in shadow and half illuminated. Then, from Edna's point of view, the vivid sky is shown.

Scene 8. Present time: Spring. Adèle's time is near.

The camera tilts down from a corner of Adèle's bedroom [Gardner, "Mooncircles"]. It is degrees darker than in the earlier scenes. Adèle sits forward in bed, head bent, supported by the nurse on one side and on the other by Edna. They gently ease Adèle back against the pillows. Adèle's face is drawn, and she is damp with perspiration. Edna and the nurse exchange glances. Adèle clenches her friend's arm. The shot changes to an image of the open window, where a light rain drops on the sill.

Scene 9. Past time: Summer. The Grand Isle dinner party.

This sequence begins with a close shot of the Pontellier cottage window viewed from the porch. Edna's hand gathers the lace curtain aside, and she peers out. Reverse angle: from her perspective the camera slides across the sloping lawn to the water oaks. There, in the dusk, two formally set dinner tables stand between two huge trees [Chopin, Waltz in G-Flat Major, Op. 70, No. 1].

Immediately the image changes, and the strong colors of a lighted Chinese lantern blurred by motion almost fill the screen. The camera pulls away to reveal MADAME LEBRUN steadying the lantern. An attractive woman, she is middle-aged, ebullient, and as always, dressed in white. She surveys the scene before her with obvious satisfaction.

It is darker now, but the scene is still well lit. The lanterns strung between the reaching tree limbs give a soft light, and mosquito torches are placed at intervals. The table settings are luxurious, all in silver, crystal, and white, with wreaths of flowers set between tall candelabra.

The camera cuts to the main house. Victor emerges on the porch, pauses, then importantly rings the bell. The parrot's screech annoys Victor, and he jostles the cage as the camera moves in for a close shot of its swinging arc. This image dissolves to a close shot of a guest's hoopskirt as it sways with a lively motion. Then with a series of random shots, somewhat matching the rhythm of couples entering a dance floor, the guests gather on the galleries. Couples arm in arm greet each other. The children race ahead; their indecipherable chatter is heard as all advance down the lawn toward the luminous banquet tables.

This series is followed by shots of the dinner in progress, all in the same rhythm, with a gradual acceleration as the spirited mood develops. Mme Lebrun presides and guides the service of elaborate trays of food. She sends a delicacy here, a pitcher of wine there, firmly directing the servants with conspicuous signals. The camera passes among the diners and catches them savoring the meal or engaged in animated conversation. It is quite noisy now, and only a word or two is heard distinctly. Only Edna seems removed; she appears attentive yet distant, even somber. At one point she fixes her gaze on a rose-mallow that has separated from its wreath. As Edna stares, it turns into a shell. Then she looks around the table, but when she returns her gaze to that spot, there is nothing there.

Now the camera pulls back as the guests stand and begin to walk up to the main house. Flickering candles highlight the disarray of the finished meal. Edna, Robert, and Léonce remain seated at angles to each other. In silence Léonce offers Robert a cigar, which he tucks away as Léonce lights up his own cigar.

A new shot: the dining hall is cleared for dancing. Green pine branches decorate the walls, chairs line the sides, the floor is polished, and the large piano occupies a prominent place. A breeze stirs the window curtains. The camera, which had been stationary, begins to move as voices are heard. As the camera rotates around the room, people appear where before there was empty space. Men stand in small groups, women bend to kiss their children goodnight, and servants fuss with chairs and finish lighting the wall lamps. *Sotto voce* Adèle speaks to the nurse while she fondly pats her children. Offscreen Mme Lebrun's voice is heard distinctly.

MME LEBRUN: Madame Ratignolle, may we prevail upon you to play?

Now Mme Lebrun is in the frame, her back to the camera. Adèle turns to face her.

ADÈLE: Oh no, (Said coyly) I'm so out of practice.
MME LEBRUN: Even so, you play with—
ADÈLE: —Well, Alphonse indulges my small talent, but—

As Adèle speaks, Mme Lebrun takes her by the arm and leads her out of the frame. The image changes to a shot of Adèle seated on the piano bench. Mme Lebrun stands alongside her.

MME LEBRUN: You play with great verve.

The voices in the room subside while the camera pulls back to show the assembled guests giving their full attention to the scene at the piano.

ADÈLE: No, not really.

MME LEBRUN: A waltz? (She nods to the guests.) Or one of the new polkas?

ALPHONSE: A waltz, my dear.

ADÈLE: (She pats herself on the stomach.) Well, if I must give up dancing, why shouldn't I play while I can still reach the keys?

There is laughter in the room. Adèle smiles happily and launches into a fast waltz [C. M. von Weber, "L' Invitation à La Valse"]. The shot changes to an image of couples as they move gaily onto the dance floor. Among the dancers are Edna and Léonce, Alphonse and Mme Lebrun, M. Farival and a young girl, the infatuated couple, and Robert and one of the young woman guests. The image quickly becomes a whirl of dancing figures, with the camera moving in and out, darting as it were, close, then back. The men move in ordered designs, intent on performing the correct steps. The women hold their open fans high and flirt in a perfunctory manner. Their wide skirts swirl and ebb like waves against the stiff, dark trousers of their partners. Edna holds her fan closed over Léonce's shoulder. Her straightforward countenance is in marked contrast to the flirtatious demeanor of the other women.

This image of the dancers dissolves into another image as they change partners. Adèle continues to play. Images of the dancers, from a further distance than in the preceding shots, are interposed with shots of Victor wheeling a wicker cart on which stands a tall silver iced cake. Behind him a maid follows with a coffee urn. The last shot is a close-up of the cake.

The image changes: Edna sits on a low windowsill, her body curved to its frame. An empty cake plate is in her lap. The music stops. Then there is a quick cut to Alphonse as he wipes Adèle's brow with his handkerchief. Next the camera returns to Edna. Robert walks into the frame and takes the dish from her lap as he asks:

ROBERT: Shall I ask Mademoiselle to play?

EDNA: A concert would be perfect, Robert. But isn't it useless to ask?

The camera angle shifts so that as Robert bends over Edna he blocks her from view.

ROBERT: If I tell her—

As Robert speaks the image dissolves to a shot of him knocking on MADEMOISELLE REISZ's door and then a shot of her walking quickly along the gallery as Robert follows. She is an older woman with an uncaring style of dress. A sprig of violets is pinned in her hair.

ROBERT: (Voice-over) She'll play for you, Mrs. Pontellier. She's so fond of you. (Pause) I'll go and ask her.

Now the two stand in the doorway of the dining hall. The camera reverses to show the surprise and pleasure of the guests. Then there is a cut back to Mademoiselle as she imperiously walks to the piano. Robert hovers over her, pushing the bench in, moving the music sheets aside. The low buzz in the room subsides.

MLLE REISZ: Ask Mrs. Pontellier what she would like to hear.

This carries in the room; nevertheless, Robert goes to Edna, who appears embarrassed by the attention. She exchanges glances with the musician. Edna speaks outwardly, as though Robert were not by her side.

EDNA: Whatever mademoiselle chooses will please me. Let her decide.

Reverse angle: Mademoiselle nods and begins to play a Chopin Etude [in C-Sharp Minor, Op. 10, No. 4]. She has the consummate skill of the dedicated professional, as well as the interpretive shadings of intellect and emotion. At the first chord the camera returns to Edna. The breeze lifts the lace curtain panel, floating it over the sill in the night air. Edna sits perfectly straight in her concentration. She is large on the screen, and her body bisects the window frame.

A new image: sheet music fills the frame. Slowly the camera pulls back to reveal the room, which is now empty, just as it was before the guests came in. Offscreen the music becomes louder and more insistent.

Now we see Edna in closeup as she looks over her shoulder to the porch. Then the camera reverses, and Edna looks directly into it. The bright lights of the dining room behind her are in sharp contrast to the dark shadows of the porch. The music stops, and Léonce's voice is heard offscreen. The camera moves further back.

LÉONCE: Coming, Edna?

She seems not to hear; she holds an unlit cigarette gracefully, motionlessly, in her lap.

Scene 10. Present time: Spring. Dr. Mandelet attends to Adèle.

This scene, which is silent and composed of erratic close shots, takes place in Adèle's bedroom. Edna stands by one side of the bed, her arms crossed, her posture tense, her eyes averted. Dr. Mandelet bends over Adèle on the other side. He administers chloroform to her with a gauze mask attached to a long, thin tube. At the other end is a dark green bottle, which is held high by the nurse. The doctor's manner has elements of contradiction; he appears solicitous, yet he also looks bored. As Dr. Mandelet attends to Adèle, shots of Adèle's disheveled hair, shadows on the wall, the empty wicker cradle, and a formal painting of Adèle are interposed. Then the image changes to Edna as she looks at Dr. Mandelet with a disturbed expression on her face. He winks over at her, and then the doctor turns and nods toward the doorway.

Scene 11. Reverie within reverie: Summer, fall. Edna and Adèle.

On an unsteady trajectory the camera moves slowly down from the top of citrus trees to the flowering bushes, then to the low plants bordering the sandy path. All the while a low murmur of voices is heard. Two figures move into the frame at extreme close shot. The camera pulls back to reveal Edna and Adèle, walking arm in arm. Adèle wears a frilly white gown, gloves, several brooches—one at her upright collar. A fan is attached to a long chain, and a bulky brocaded bag is fastened to her waist with pink ribbons. A lacy hat completes the costume. Edna's tailored white dress has a thin vertical lavender stripe. She wears her straw hat. Adèle holds one side of her skirt over her arm, but this is just a gesture, as both their skirts trail in the sand. In a moment, but after they have walked like this for what seems like a longer period, the familiar sounds of the beach mingle with their voices. A new shot finds them arranging themselves on an Oriental rug laid in front of the Ratignolle bathhouse. Large pillows lean against the porch footings. Both women sit with their skirts tucked under their legs. Adèle adjusts her face veil and arranges her sewing materials. She leans back into the half shadow that falls from the porch. Edna holds sketching materials in her lap. She tilts her face up to the full sun; her eyes are closed. With her profile large in the left foreground of the screen, she lowers her face to look around. Then from Edna's perspective the camera makes an arc across the beach. Several guests stand by the shore; others play in the surf, which seems more billowy than before; the infatuated couple sit under a large tent; the elderly widow leans over her porch rail, and her necklace cross falls forward. Edna turns to look at Adèle, and the camera moves to the side so that the field of the image encompasses the background of the shore. Adèle secures her hat with a large pin. Edna removes hers, and long strands of hair escape from her thick chignon and blow about her face. Adèle idly opens her orange fan. Edna unbuttons her collar and wrist cuffs.

ADÈLE: Chérie, be careful, you'll burn!
EDNA: Just like Léonce. Are we so fragile?

Adèle pats the shaded spot next to her on the rug, but Edna doesn't notice. She is engrossed by the sea.

ADÈLE: In this heat, one must be careful. (Long pause) You look so serious, Edna. Are you thinking?
EDNA: This is so beautiful. I should try to capture it. (Pause) Am I thinking? Not really. Yet thoughts—I just want—

She takes the fan from Adèle and alternates fanning them both vigorously. For a brief moment Edna holds the fan up to her face.

EDNA: Well, how can I put it? Notions come into my head.
ADÈLE: Ah, if it's private, ma belle.

The camera slowly turns, panning down to the shore and pausing where the waves break. The sun's glare is intensely felt. It is as though the scene is drenched by the heat of summer. Then the field of the image is enlarged to include several fishing boats in the distance. Far in the left background are the shapes of several small fir-covered islands.

EDNA: (Offscreen) I would like to talk. Lately thoughts go racing through my mind.
ADÈLE: It is much too hot to think.

Reverse angle: on the two women again. Edna puts the fan down and Adèle picks it up.

EDNA: Yes. But for the fun of it, Adèle.

During this next series of shots Adèle and Edna will continue to speak, but offscreen; then it falls silent. The image changes to a room that is shadowy and vague in detail. It has a homespun aspect. Several people stand in the background. TWO LITTLE GIRLS, one quite still, the other restless, sit on a bench. Between them is Edna, exactly as she was on the beach. The mood is somber. A TALL STERN MAN is the focus of the shot. He reads dramatically from a large Bible. A couple who had been in the background come forward to greet the girls. The woman pats them awkwardly, and the man shakes hands with them, after which Edna rises suddenly; she moves just as a child hoping to be undetected might and edges out of the room. Offscreen dialogue is heard.

EDNA: I've heard from my sister Janet. She's to be married.
ADÈLE: How wonderful! A wedding.
EDNA: Do you really think so, Adèle?
ADÈLE: Let me go with you when you order your gown. There's a new salon—outside the Quarter, but they say it is très chic.

As Edna departs from the room a slow fade introduces the next sequence of shots. Edna is in an open field of tall grain. She still wears the dress of the beach scene and is tying the strings of a large sunbonnet. The barley is so tall that she must reach her arms out to part the stalks and walk forward. The atmosphere is hushed and expectant. The camera moves in close. Edna stops and looks back as though she hears someone call to her. The image changes to a shot of the older of the two little girls on a rustic porch as she waves a "come back" motion in vain. The camera returns to Edna. She rhythmically propels her arms forward to clear a path through the field. Offscreen her voice is heard.

EDNA: I rarely think of my old home. Except when my father reminds me of our Kentucky horses. But it comes back to me today. My mother, so still . . . her ivory comb. I wish I had kept it.

Then, as Edna's arm comes up in an arc, the shot dissolves to her arm coming down lightly on Adèle's shoulder. The two are just as they were before, together on the beach rug in front of the bathhouse, except that Edna is now closer to Adèle. The camera moves back and up. It almost looks down over the top of Edna's head.

EDNA: There was a vast, or so it seemed to me then, green field close to my home. I used to wander there, idly, unthinking, unguided. Content, yet always looking back—making certain to keep our roof in view. It's clear to me—

Adèle clasps Edna's hand firmly in hers; with the other she strokes her friend's arm. Edna looks pleased. She goes on as the image shifts to a side angle.

EDNA: Perhaps it's even more real to me than this island. Yet, the absence—
ADÈLE: My poor Chérie.
EDNA: When I close my eyes all I see are waves.

Edna leans her head on Adèle's shoulder. Her face is flushed. The field of the image enlarges now to include the shore and the sea. The sun's sparkle on the water gives an impression of unending wavy lines.

Off camera the sounds of approaching voices are heard. The lower half of Robert's body is large in the frame in the foreground. Then the Pontellier and Ratignolle children walk into view. The camera angle changes to show Edna and Adèle as they look up at Robert and the children. Then the angle reverses to Robert. He has Adèle's little girl in his arms. Robert kneels and releases the child. The children scamper off; the two nurses follow.

A new shot: Edna walks alone down to the shore and the camera follows at a distance. Offscreen Adèle speaks:

ADÈLE: We were like two young girls. I didn't touch my sewing. (Pause) We just talked. About nothing, really. (Pause) Will you be an angel—

The camera turns back to Adèle and Robert and comes in close as they both rise.

ADÈLE: —Robert, and walk me to the cottage?
ROBERT: It is my pleasure to serve you. (He bows.)
ADÈLE: (Takes him by the arm) What would we all do without you?

Scene 12. Prophecy: The birth.

A woman's humming is heard. It is a melody that has a lovely and emphatic quality [Gardner, "Winter Night, Gibbous Moon"]. A narrow waterway in the bayou countryside appears. Low-hanging branches reach across the still, dark water. In a moment a long flat-boat edges into the top of the screen and glides smoothly through the water. Its image is reflected in the water. Several women of different races and ages serve as crew. One woman holds a baby wrapped in soft rainbow hues. The image changes to a shot of Adèle on the shore of a small inlet in the bayou. She stands erect and calm. Other women wait with her. Their shadows undulate on the water. The boat glides to shore, and someone throws a line. There is a quick cut to an onlooker's reaching arm as she skillfully catches the rope.

Scene 13. Present time: Spring. Edna returns to the "little house."

A new shot: Adèle's nurse is seen in the shadows of the bedroom. She holds an infant wrapped in a beige blanket in her arms. It is she who is humming. The camera turns to the bed where an exhausted Adèle lies, clutching a handkerchief. Edna walks into the frame. She is tired also; tendrils of hair lie damp on her cheek. Edna waves her hand over Adèle to dispense the fumes.
The image changes. Edna stands by the window; the camera is behind her. She leans forward in the open window, her arms braced on the sill. After a moment, she turns her face into the room, then

she goes to Adèle as the camera moves back. Edna kisses her friend lightly.

ADÈLE: (Weakly) Edna, my baby. (Pause) She's so beautiful—so fair. Did you see her?
EDNA: Yes. You must rest, Adèle.
ADÈLE: The children, Edna, the children.

Adèle's eyes close; Edna turns to leave. As the camera remains on Adèle, we hear the indistinct tones of a jovial conversation in the hall. The masculine voices are Alphonse's and Dr. Mandelet's. Only an occasional word is clear, such as "mayor," "rascals," and "the levee." Here there is a quick cut to the open window. Now the humming stops.

A new shot, framed from above the dimly lit hallway. Edna, the doctor, and Alphonse descend the narrow stairway. As they arrive at the vestibule, the two step aside to let Edna pass. Alphonse bends to kiss her hand, and then he turns to the doctor and gives him an affectionate hug. The image changes: Edna and the doctor stand together outside the open doorway. Then the camera pulls back to reveal the street scene.

The French Quarter street of the Ratignolle home is very old. Alphonse's apothecary is on the first floor. The cobblestoned road is lined with tall, narrow townhouses. The lingering wetness that follows a New Orleans rainfall brings a light mist, yet the sky is now clear and starry. At the curb, a coupé and driver wait. The horse softly paws the ground.

The camera remains at a distance and to the right. Edna wraps her fringed shawl around her and starts off. Dr. Mandelet calls to her, and the two pause in conversation on the sidewalk. Then he turns and waves the driver on. The two walk on together. The only sound is the sound of their steps on the wet pavement. A series of alternating shots accompanies them; there are angled shots from the side of their earnest conversational pose, then closer shots of their striding legs, and all the while, a slowly running rivulet of curb water is seen in the image. These shots come to a stop when they reach the gate of Edna's "little house." All that is visible in the dark of this scene is a high brick wall and a tall ironwork gate capped with an ornate oval design.

Dr. Mandelet takes a wide stance with his walking stick, which he holds in both hands and leans on.

DR. MANDELET: When does Léonce return?

EDNA: (Her arms are folded in the shawl.) Quite soon.

DR. MANDELET: You seem troubled, Edna. Come and see me, we'll have a talk.

EDNA: (She looks offscreen.) If only one might go on dreaming—

The doctor's coach pulls up in front of the walk. Dr. Mandelet signals the driver with his cane. Then there is a close shot of Edna as she entwines her fingers through the design of the gate.

DR. MANDELET: (Offscreen) I would understand, and I tell you there are not many who would.

EDNA: But to wake up and find—

Edna shrugs and opens the gate. She continues:

EDNA: There are moods which overtake me. I don't feel moved to speak. (Pause) You are kind, dear Dr. Mandelet. Good night.

The image changes to a shot of the doctor as he boards his coach. He leans out and waves as the coach moves out of the frame. The horse and carriage sounds are muted. The camera returns to Edna. She stands on the path inside the gate looking out. Behind her a light shines through a front window. In a toneless voice she says to herself:

EDNA: "Yet do the shades come without the sun."

She looks boldly into the camera and then turns as the shot fades.

ACT II

Scene 1. Present time: Spring. Edna finds Robert gone.

The camera faces into the cozy parlor of Edna's "little house" from the front doorway. It is late in the evening, and the room is lit by candlelight. There is a pleasant array of tasteful pictures, books, and

Edna's painting materials. Small Oriental rugs lie over the floor matting. Just visible in the background is a tiny dining room that looks crowded with a small buffet and table. The camera angle changes to a shot of Edna's narrow, booted feet on the threshold. Then there is a quick cut to Edna's hand as she reaches for a note propped against a framed photograph of herself. Edna's face is dimly reflected in its glass [Guiraud, "Sylvia"]. The camera moves back to reveal Edna's trancelike motions as she sits on the settee and arranges the pillows against the arm before lying down. This side of the room is shadowy. Her eyes scan the wall and come to rest on a small watercolor. The camera draws close to this seascape until the painting fills the screen. This closeup gives it an appearance of an actual beach. Then the camera shifts slightly to show the frame.

Scene 2. Past time: Summer. Léonce leaves for the city and Edna paints.

This next series of shots begins with a pan of the sandy parkway of the Lebrun Hotel. The camera pauses, and a horse's tail flicks across the frame. Then the camera pulls back to the middle distance to reveal two rockaways in front of the porch, one in front of the other. The driver of one hoists several brocaded bags to the luggage rack. The camera pulls back even further. Guests lounge on the porch or stand by the rail. The clink and murmur of a meal being cleared drift out to the parkway. Adèle stands with Alphonse at the top of the porch stairs. She holds her youngest child snugly in her arms. Alphonse bends over them and pumps the toddler's tiny arm. Now the shot changes to a view of Léonce pacing up the parkway, with Raoul and Etienne tumbling about him. The nurse follows in the background. As the camera turns to face the scene in front of the porch, they stop in front of the second rockaway. The first has already boarded passengers.

RAOUL: This time don't forget the caramels.

ETIENNE: From Boule's. You promised.

LÉONCE: (He kisses each child.) Yes, yes. Be good boys while I'm gone.

During this exchange several of the women guests have joined them on the parkway.

FIRST GUEST: Have a good week, Monsieur Pontellier. We'll miss you.

SECOND GUEST: We'll keep Edna occupied.

Léonce boards the rockaway and looks at his watch.

LÉONCE: Well, business as usual.

Now Alphonse walks into the frame.

ALPHONSE: If it were not so stifling in the city.

The camera pulls further back to show more of this tableau. Alphonse turns to throw kisses to Adèle. At this moment Edna walks into the frame. She leans over the porch rail and smiles and waves to the two men. The first rockaway starts off. Alphonse joins Léonce in the second. Then Adèle rushes down the stairs to clasp her husband's hand as he reaches out to her. Léonce leans over him and calls out to Edna in a teasing manner:

LÉONCE: Edna, when I return, will you have become a graceful mermaid of the sea?

Everyone laughs in recognition of this sally. The camera moves close to Edna to show her blush. She nervously pokes a slender finger through the thick waves of her hair.

The camera remains on Edna. We hear the second rockaway start off with the sounds of its light-wheeled rustle on sand and the pita-pat of the spirited mare.

LÉONCE: Adieu, my loves.

Edna turns and walks out of the frame. Abruptly the image changes to a rear view of M. Farival, who hurries along the parkway after the retreating carriage. He shouts ineffectually as the image fades out in a cloud of the carriage's dust:

M. FARIVAL: Your wife—if she will only follow my instructions—

A new shot: the camera peers through the lacy wood trim of the hotel gazebo. It is midafternoon. Adèle is doing her embroidery.

Edna has her easel set up and is sketching Adèle. Robert watches Edna draw from his vantage point on the top step. The camera slides across to the entranceway so that the gazebo trim becomes a border of the frame.

ROBERT: (To Edna) Your talent is immense!
ADÈLE: I've always thought so.

Robert leans against Edna, but she pulls away without comment. It is quiet for a moment. Then Edna speaks with exasperation.

EDNA: (She stops work.) This is not what I intended. Not at all.

The camera tilts over the drawing. Edna and Robert are partially in the frame. Again, Robert leans on Edna, and just as before, she moves away from the pressure of his body. The camera returns to the position of the preceding shot. Adèle looks up.

ADÈLE: May I see it now?
EDNA: (Still annoyed) Ah, why go on?

She takes the brush and obliterates her drawing with broad angry strokes. Then she crumples the sketch and lets it fall to the floor. Robert and Adèle exchange glances. Edna starts to pack up her paint box.

ROBERT: Shall I see if tea is ready?

Scene 3. Present time: Spring. Edna, lost in thought.

As Robert speaks the image dissolves into a shot of Edna in the "little house."

ADÈLE: (Offscreen) Is it time?

Edna lies on the settee just as she was in the earlier shot (act 2, scene 1). Now she holds an unfurled rough sketch in front of her. While the subject is vague, it appears to be an outline of a head in profile. All during this brief scene phrases of piano music that we have heard before are played, particularly the melodies from Mlle Reisz's concert [Chopin, Etude in C-Sharp Minor, Op. 10, No. 4]. The camera passes across a section of the parlor and stops just behind Edna's head so that the upheld sketch is large in the frame. Then the camera moves even closer to eliminate all of the background. The whiteness of the sketch becomes the image, and this dissolves into a large sunny room.

Scene 4. Reverie: Summer. A Series: The letter, the night swimming.

The large sunny room is Mme Lebrun's dormer room. The interior reflects the sloping ceiling and angled attic shapes. Two windows overlook the lawn. In the distance is the sea. The room's sparse light oak furniture and white accessories give it an airy look. Family photographs abound. The one incongruous element is a clumsy-looking sewing machine set at a right angle to a front window. Immediately the loud racket of the machine is heard. Mme Lebrun sews with power supplied by the little black girl, who crouches underneath to move the pedals by hand.

EDNA: (Offscreen) Good morning.

Mme Lebrun does not stop, but she is delighted to see Edna.

MME LEBRUN: My dear Mrs. Pontellier, how charming you look—and so rosy. Have you been neglecting your veil?

During this last sentence Edna moves into the frame and takes a seat on the wide window bench.

EDNA: Have you heard from Robert?
MME LEBRUN: A letter arrived in yesterday's packet. (She stops the machine.) He reminds me to give you a certain book. (She looks under the machine.) Delice, go and fetch it. (As the child runs out) Look next to the lamp in Monsieur Robert's room.
EDNA: It must be the Goncourt. He was reading it to Adèle and me. (Pause) May I see the letter?

Mme Lebrun takes a letter from her large apron pocket and hands it to Edna.

MME LEBRUN: Of course.

As Edna starts to read to herself, Mme Lebrun continues to speak with her usual animation.

MME LEBRUN: He says he had a drink with Mr. Pontellier before departing. Your husband thinks his prospects in Mexico are excellent. Robert says he had a fine trip. It did him good. He'll write again soon. Mrs. Pontellier?

During Mme Lebrun's monologue the camera moves in closer to her and eliminates Edna from the screen. As she says "Mrs. Pontellier?" the image changes to a shot of Mme Lebrun in a different setting. It is evening, and some of the guests have gathered on the hotel's large porch. The camera pulls back to reveal, in addition to Mme Lebrun, the Ratignolles, Léonce, Robert, and one of the other guests. They leisurely sip coffee around a small table. That section of the porch is well lighted, but the rest is dark and shadowy. Mme Lebrun continues to speak, almost without pause.

MME LEBRUN: Ah, here comes our Mrs. Pontellier.

Edna walks into the frame and seats herself slightly to the rear of the others.

EDNA: Excuse me. Please continue, Robert.
ROBERT: I'm afraid I was boring everyone.
GUEST: Oh, no. Not at all.
LÉONCE: We Creoles are too bold for my wife.
EDNA: (Mme Lebrun hands her a cup of coffee.) So it's on my account.
ROBERT: It's only a little gossip about Alcée Arobin.
ADÈLE: (Her tone is arch.) He's not a gentleman.
MME LEBRUN: Why, do you recall a Madame Bénoite? They were seen together everywhere.
ADÈLE: (She reaches over to pat Robert on the arm.) Quite unlike our Robert.

During Robert's response the camera slides away from the group and pauses at Edna. From her perspective it will pass across the lawn until the dark shapes of the water oaks loom up. The full moon casts patterns through the draped Spanish moss of the trees. After a pause the conversation continues offscreen.

ROBERT: I am just a seasonal amusement. A feature of the program.

FIRST GUEST: We all recall your devotion to Madame Duvigné, and last year it was Mrs. Ratignolle, and this summer it's Mrs. Pontellier.

ADÈLE: Par exemple! I never had to ask. You were always there.

ROBERT: Just until Ratignolle appeared on the scene, then it was "out with you."

ADÈLE: Perhaps I feared to make Alphonse jealous.

An outburst of laughter greets this sally. It is followed by a quick cut to Edna's profile. The camera pulls back as Adèle and Alphonse clasp hands across the table. Edna's face is clear, but her hands, which rest under her chin, are blurred. Now the camera turns to Mme Lebrun.

MME LEBRUN: Robert, think of something for us to do—something frivolous, perhaps?

The shot changes: the field of the image widens to include the whole group, even the front steps and some portion of the parkway.

ROBERT: I've already thought of it. Why don't we go down to the shore for a cooling dip?

MME LEBRUN: Marvelous! (She rises.) With this moon, it's even light enough.

LÉONCE: But it's so late.

The others stand up and begin slowly and deliberately to walk down the stairs.

ADÈLE: It will be a tonic.

Edna and Robert smile at each other. Now Léonce follows the others. Alphonse pauses on the shadowy parkway. He motions the others to halt and speaks oratorically:

ALPHONSE: Next winter when the wind's icy breath blows through our chimneys, we will remember this lovely night.

Midway through the sentence the image changes. We see the

guests in their bathing costumes; they move dreamlike into the shallow water. Alphonse's voice becomes quite dim at the end. M. Farival, Victor, and the infatuated couple have joined the swimming party. Torches have been placed at intervals along the shore. Their flickering light reaches out to the long narrow beams of moonlight on the water. Now Robert enters the frame from the background. He carries a folding chair, which he places at the edge of the shore for Léonce. From the distance, gay strains of a band waft across to them [Gottschalk, "Tarantelle"]. The men in the water move further out; the women stay closer to shore in a little group. Léonce sits; Robert stands next to him. Both men light cigarettes, and the night breeze carries the puffs of smoke across the screen.

The camera turns seaward to focus on Edna, who is off by herself. She splashes about, in imitation of a swimmer's motions. After a moment, she appears to be floating. Edna stops, then she stands, and the camera moves in close. Now she immerses herself again, tentatively stroking the water. With a quick look of joy she rises and turns toward shore. Then once more, she strokes through the water, swimming in a little circle. After several turns, Edna stands and shouts toward shore:

EDNA: I can swim! I'm swimming!

The camera turns and frames the scene on shore much like a still photograph.

ROBERT: Wonderful, Mrs. Pontellier.
M. FARIVAL: (He turns to the others.) It's just as I predicted.
MME LEBRUN: (To M. Farival) It was Robert who had the patience.
   (She calls to Edna.) Very good, my dear, you've a natural style.
LÉONCE: Don't get chilled, Edna.

At this last remark, the camera turns back to observe Edna plunging into the calm sea and swimming out a bit further. The music fades away. The camera advances with a down tilt above the water. In a closeup it follows Edna as she pulls herself through the water. The sounds of her breathing and the water's flow are very distinct and obvious. After a long moment she lifts her head and looks back to shore. Her eyes show fear. Turning with floundering strokes, she marshals her strength and swims somewhat awkwardly toward shore. When she reaches the shallows, Edna rises and stands there to regain her breath. The camera angle reverses: Léonce stands by on shore with Edna's bathrobe open in front of him.

The shot changes to an image of Edna on shore wrapped in the long robe. Léonce pats her face dry with a small towel.

EDNA: I thought I might perish out there.
LÉONCE: You were not out so very far, Edna. I was watching you.
EDNA: It's a wonderful sensation. Nonetheless—I felt (She moves Léonce's arm away.) Like . . . like . . . A . . .
LÉONCE: You're trembling, Edna. Are you chilled, my dear?

Edna turns and walks toward the bathhouses. Léonce's back is to the camera as the shot fades out.

Now the soft chords of a guitar are heard. The camera pans a short distance along the shore to a large tent with its flaps rolled up. The Lebrun guests lounge inside. Victor plays a romantic French ballad, "Ah! Si Tu Savais," on his guitar. Everyone begins to sing in accompaniment.

After a moment the camera pulls back to reveal Edna's shadowy figure in the background of the screen; she has changed back into her gown and walks slowly toward the path.

MME LEBRUN: (She calls to Edna.) Stay and join us.
ADÈLE: Edna, you have such a lovely voice—stay—

Léonce joins the others under the tent. Edna turns to them and waves. She shakes her head "no" and walks out of the frame. The camera moves closer to the group under the tent as Mme Lebrun speaks to Léonce.

MME LEBRUN: I'm tempted to think that your wife is capricious.
LÉONCE: Sometimes. Not often.

The camera cuts to the path, which is well lit by the full moon. Edna's gown is large in the frame; the hem trails along the sand. Then footsteps and the rustle of plants are heard. Edna turns to see who it is as the camera moves back to a long shot. Robert walks into the frame. He has hurried to catch up with Edna. They stand still for a brief moment.

EDNA: Did you think I was afraid?

The two walk on side by side, in a series of shots that alternate between their faces in profile and long shots as the camera tracks ahead of them. The pair converse as they walk on and we hear the soft buzz of insects in the background.

ROBERT: No, I knew you weren't.
EDNA: (She holds the damp coils of her hair.) I am trying to think.
ROBERT: Shall I go back to the others?
EDNA: No—stay—I'm just tired tonight.
ROBERT: I know you are.
EDNA: (Annoyed) You don't know anything about it, why should you? (Softer) A thousand emotions have swept through me tonight.

As Edna speaks, her voice becomes more confident, even though her words seem vague. Also, her stance seems taller.

EDNA: Even I don't understand half of them.

They walk on in silence for a moment. Robert pauses to snap a flower from its stem.

EDNA: Don't mind what I say. This night is like a dream. (Pause) Everything seems unreal to me.
ROBERT: Perhaps it's because there are spirits abroad.

The camera angle changes: the branches hang over Edna and Robert like a reaching canopy. Only the tops of their heads are visible through the dark mesh of leaves.

EDNA: What do you mean, Robert?
ROBERT: On this very night a spirit that has always haunted these shores seeks someone worthy of its spell. Tonight it has found Edna.
EDNA: Don't banter.

A new shot: Edna and Robert reach the Pontellier cottage. Edna sits in the hammock in the foreground; Robert lounges against the tree. It is quite dark, yet shapes and certain details are clear. The gable corner of the main house shows its odd angles; the dormer window is heavily draped.

ROBERT: Will you stay out here and wait for Mr. Pontellier?

During this sentence Edna stretches out in the hammock and settles herself comfortably.

EDNA: I'll wait out here. (Pause) Good night, Robert.
ROBERT: Shall I bring you a pillow?
EDNA: I have one. (It's not in view.)

Edna puts her hand to the ground and gives the hammock a gentle sway as Robert walks off. From Edna's perspective we view Robert as he passes in and out of the strips of moonlight. The field of the image widens as Robert walks slowly out of the frame. Now the image shifts to an angled foreground shot of Edna's crossed feet at the tip of the hammock. The muffled voices of the returning swimming party are heard offscreen, as well as a chord of the guitar and a tired laugh. Then all is quiet.

Now the camera shifts to Léonce as he starts up the porch stairs. Then he catches sight of Edna in the hammock.

LÉONCE: Edna, what are you doing? I thought you went to bed.

There is no answer. Léonce walks over to the hammock and bends over Edna to see if she's asleep. The camera angle changes so that the hammock is horizontal in the frame. Léonce's form casts a shadow over Edna.

LÉONCE: Are you asleep? (He straightens up.)

The camera angle shifts to Edna's face; her eyes shine with an unnatural light as she looks up at Léonce.

EDNA: No.
LÉONCE: (Offscreen) It's very late, Edna. (Pause) I'm going in to bed.

The image changes to a shot of Léonce in his nightclothes, as he looks through the curtained doorway.

LÉONCE: Edna?

Léonce comes out on the porch and stands at the top of the stairs.

He sips a glass of wine. The camera moves back so that both Léonce and Edna are in the field of the image.

LÉONCE: You'll take cold out there.
EDNA: It isn't cold. (Her eyes are closed.)
LÉONCE: The mosquitoes will devour you. (His temper flares.) What folly is this?

Léonce turns in a huff and goes inside. We hear him move about in the cottage. Then Léonce comes to the doorway.

LÉONCE: (Placatingly) Edna, dear, are you coming in soon?
EDNA: (She looks up to the porch and speaks with determination.) No, Léonce. I'm staying out here.
LÉONCE: (He comes out on the porch again, and his voice is low with anger, but even.) This is more than folly. I won't permit it. You must come in.

While Léonce speaks, Edna twists her body in the hammock as though to secure her place there. The camera view shifts to almost underneath the hammock, and holds steady, as the hammock sways.

EDNA: (She speaks firmly.) I don't wish to come in, Léonce. Go to bed. And don't speak to me like that again.

It is quiet. The camera turns somewhat haltingly toward Edna, where it pauses for a moment and then turns back to the porch with the same uncertain movement. There Léonce sits in the rocker and smokes a cigar, with his slippered feet up on the rail. Night sounds are heard—perhaps the meow of a cat, or an owl's call. With a slow dissolve the image returns to Edna. She hasn't moved; she looks stiff. This shot is held for a long moment, even a monotonous moment. Then she sits up and rises unsteadily and drowsily.
    The shot changes: Edna stands in the porch doorway. She hesitates, and then turns to Léonce as she rests her arm on the doorway, which partly blocks her face. Finally she speaks:

EDNA: Are you coming in, Léonce?

The camera turns to Léonce, who is just about to light another cigar. He waits and takes his first puff, and then as he exhales the smoke,

LÉONCE: Yes, dear. Just as soon as I finish my smoke.

The final image of this scene is the thin smoke as it dissolves in the night air.

Scene 5. Past time: Winter. Edna visits Adèle in town.

This scene begins in the front hall of the Pontellier's New Orleans residence. Léonce is preparing to leave, carefully adjusting his hat in front of the mirror stand, selecting a walking stick, tucking a port-folio under his arm. The camera comes in close as he opens the door to the veranda.

Then the shot dissolves into an image of Edna's hand on the ban-ister of the wide, curving hall stairway. As Edna descends the stairs, the viewer glimpses the furnishings. They reflect Léonce's monied position and his French taste. There are plush, deeply dyed fabrics on the sofas and chairs, heavy Oriental carpets, dark carved wood trims, large ferns, tall urns, and a wall of gilt-framed paintings. When Edna reaches the bottom of the stairs, the camera follows her onto the veranda.

The shot changes: Edna and Léonce stand together on the veranda. They are viewed from a curbside vantage point. A portion of the waiting carriage can be seen in the frame.

LÉONCE: Care to meet me in town, Edna? I've decided to improve the library. (He waits for her to answer.) What do you think of the new gasoliers? I hear the Belthrops have placed an order.
EDNA: New fixtures, Léonce! You're far too extravagant.

Léonce starts to respond, but then he pauses to give Edna a per-functory kiss. He strides down to the carriage; his words trail behind him.

LÉONCE: The way to become rich is to make money, my dear Edna, not to save it. (Pause) And I intend for us to be rich.

Edna waves; she is unsmiling. The camera slides away to a side perspective. Léonce enters the carriage; as he pulls the door closed, an elegantly embossed "P" can be seen on its exterior. Léonce calls up to Edna:

LÉONCE: You look pale, Edna. Rest in bed today.

The shot fades. Then there is a close shot of Edna in profile on the veranda as she leans forward against the trellis. She is pensive. From the background we hear the sounds of Raoul and Etienne being pulled in a wagon around the veranda. There is only a glimpse of the nurse as she passes behind Edna. Then the sounds of the boys and the wagon fade out [John Beach, "Orleans Alley"]. Suddenly the everyday noise of the street becomes apparent; in a heavily accented voice a fruit vendor calls, "Fresh pineapples today." The camera angle shifts so that Edna is partially obscured by the vine.

Edna appears with the same pensive expression, except now as the camera pulls away she is in her atelier; it is a large, almost bare room. There are painting supplies on a long narrow oak table, a small chair or two, the easel and a stool, and some sketches, which lean against the walls. The windows are tall and very narrow; fan-lights are placed between them. Edna moves restlessly around the room. At one point she bends to examine one of the stacked canvases. Suddenly, a gramophone appears that we had not noticed earlier. The camera draws close, and we see Edna's hands in the frame as she cranks the machine [Guiraud, "Sylvia"]. A moment later there is a knock on the door.

THE MAID: Madame, are you in there?

Halfway through this sentence, the image changes to Edna on the street with a large shawl wrapped around her and a cumbersome leather sketch portfolio under her arm. The camera stalks Edna through the narrow, crowded, labyrinthine streets of the old French Quarter. By alternation the camera first follows her at a distance and then views her in closeup as she makes her way along. A sense of haphazard industry pervades the scene. Stall vendors call their wares; sailors in foreign uniforms walk in twos and threes; gentlemen in capes and tall hats walk by; servant women carry their large, heavy loads balanced on their heads or in panniers. Edna walks with an eager bearing. She is aware of her surroundings yet somehow emotionally removed from the atmosphere of the Quarter. This tracking sequence continues for a long duration. As it ends, there is a sudden darting close shot of a YOUNG BOY with a large basket. He tugs at Edna's skirt and calls:

YOUNG BOY: Now is the time to buy my pretty lavender. Now is the . . .

A new shot: Edna stands in a vestibule viewed from the middle distance. From inside the frosted glass door a maid appears to admit Edna. The room is a large and airy parlor, with the atmosphere of a sun porch. One long wall is of French doors open to a second-story balcony. The color of pale blue is everywhere, and large bowls of roses are carefully arranged. The maid leaves, and the camera moves in closer. In a moment Adèle rushes in and exclaims:

ADÈLE: I am so pleased to see you, chérie.

The two embrace fondly. Adèle's pregnancy is highlighted by an empire gown. She draws her friend to a couch.

ADÈLE: It's so tiring, this having to stay at home. But Alphonse insists.
EDNA: He is the best of husbands, Adèle.
ADÈLE: And so is Léonce. He spoils you, but who would not?

Edna has picked up a stereoscope from the tea table. Selecting a card she looks at the view while Adèle continues:

ADÈLE: I heard that you were seen walking alone the other after-noon. On the levee. "What can my dear friend be thinking of?" I wondered.

Edna puts the stereoscope in her lap, and the camera comes in close as the card slips out. It is a view of the Eiffel Tower. Edna's response begins offscreen, then as the camera pulls back, both women are in the image from a side angle.

EDNA: Is it so strange that I take walks? I enjoy myself.
ADÈLE: But unescorted?
EDNA: (She takes another card for the stereoscope.) We women, Adèle, what chance have we of learning about—
ADÈLE: It's not that, my dove, I worry about you. Perhaps—

The camera moves in front of the couch to show the two women in long shot. Edna good humoredly interrupts; she reaches for her portfolio.

EDNA: But look, Adèle, I came to get your advice. I'm painting seriously now.

ADÈLE: (Flattered) Heavens, you're asking me? I'm far—

EDNA: (Speaking rather fast) I value your opinion. Now tell me. (She arranges several of the sketches on and around the table.) What do you think? I've been to see the dealer Laidpore, and he thinks he can sell my sketches. I may even take lessons again. "Why not try?" I ask myself.

ADÈLE: Why I've always admired your talent. But what will people say? And whatever does Léonce think?

EDNA: (Sadly) He thinks I neglect my duties.

ADÈLE: Surely not! You never do.

Adèle dreamily takes a rose from the bowl and sweeps the petals lightly across Edna's cheek. Edna rises and walks out of the frame. The image shifts to her as she stands by the open French doors. She turns toward Adèle and places her hands behind her on the door knob.

EDNA: Must we always think of what others will say? What harm can there be if I work on my sketches? People like them. It pleases me.

There is a moment of silence, then Adèle speaks:

ADÈLE: (Offscreen) Why not consult Mademoiselle Reisz? (With respect) She is an artist.

At this moment, the camera pulls back, and Alphonse enters the room. He takes off his pharmaceutical coat, greets Edna with a kiss on her hand, and then as he goes to Adèle, speaks over his shoulder:

ALPHONSE: Mrs. Pontellier, you're staying for lunch?

ADÈLE: (She rises to embrace Alphonse.) Of course she'll stay. We won't let her leave.

The image changes to a shot of Edna and the Ratignolles from the rear, as they firmly lead her between them through the wide doors of the dining room.

This next series of shots is of the three at lunch, which is rather formal. The tone is a static, evenly paced sequence of fragmented shots of the serving, eating, and conversation. The first shot is of Alphonse, with his soup spoon held aloft, as he stares at Edna. The maid will serve the course and stand by.

ALPHONSE: You're not looking as well as usual.
EDNA: I feel quite well. In fact, I feel very well.

Adèle nods affirmatively as Alphonse continues:

ALPHONSE: Just the same, I am going to prepare a tonic for you, and I will not let you leave without it.

It is quiet for a moment. Edna does not seem interested in the lunch. She makes stilted motions with the food while she studies Adèle and Alphonse. They continue with an animated conversation. The next course is served.

ALPHONSE: Is Mr. Pontellier still planning to go to New York? Business improves every day! (He pauses to take a bite.) I told Adèle that Mayor Shakspeare is as good as his word.
ADÈLE: For once!
ALPHONSE: It takes time. This new crowd has the right idea. This filet is excellent, Adèle. Edna, try some more. The talk is that there's a move under way to circulate another petition against the lottery. About time!
ADÈLE: Ah, those ruffians. What would they do for mischief without the lottery?

At these words the camera pulls back in a steady trajectory through the rooms of the Ratignolle apartment, out through the vestibule, and then fades. Simultaneously the muffled voices of Adèle and Alphonse are heard from a distance.

Scene 6. Present time: Spring. Edna at the Pontellier house.

During this scene the camera tracks Edna as she returns to the Pontellier house. It is dusky and silent. Edna walks into the frame wearing the costume of the "long night." As she turns a corner there is the vaguely seen foliage and tall ironwork fence of the yard. Then as Edna walks across the veranda we notice a shuttered window and then a door, which becomes large in the frame. Next we see the interior hallway and the staircase as Edna goes upstairs. The last shot is of Edna as she cautiously pushes a door open. The outlines of her bedroom are barely visible in the dim predawn light.

Scene 7. Reverie within reverie: Winter/Summer. Dream or daydream, Chênière Caminada.

It is early evening. Edna's bedroom is well lit. It is a beautiful room with tasteful furnishings that reflect a subdued Victorian-American mode. The pale yellow-and-pink flower pattern wallpaper is a prominent feature of the room. One of the exceptional pieces of furniture is a chaise of light wood and tailored print fabric that juts out into the room. There are several large mirrors. One hangs over the fireplace. We first take note of Edna as the camera moves back. She leans against a corner of the mantelpiece, wearing a blue peignoir with wide sleeves and loose contours. Her face is turned toward the mirror, and her reflection is distinct, yet her actual image appears blurred as though the reflection is independent of Edna. Throughout this scene unobtrusive piano music is heard [Theodore Von La Hace, "By the Banks of the River"].

The camera angle shifts: Edna languidly walks over to her desk. Seated there, she stares at a blank sheet of paper. Suddenly agitated, she rises and almost knocks over the chair. Going to the balcony door she opens it and glances outside. Nervously Edna pokes her finger through her hair. She turns and paces back and forth in a way that reflects her image at varying angles in the several mirrors.

After a moment Edna returns to the open door and walks out onto the balcony. She leans over the rail. It is very dark, but one can make out the tangled limbs and intertwined vines of the tropical garden below. With great effort Edna reaches for a tree branch and pulls it toward her, leisurely breathing in the scent of blossoms. The sound of the branch snapping back is quite loud.

The shot changes: Edna lies across the top of her bed, her head nestled in the pillows. She idly traces the curving design of the inlaid enamel trim of her bedside table. As the camera draws closer, we notice her wedding band, and then, so does she. With only her arm, the side of the table, and a section of the bed in view, Edna removes the ring. The camera angle shifts slightly as Edna gropes for the camellia, which is on the coverlet; she locates it and slips the ring over the stem. Then, with an absent-minded gesture she slides the ring over the stem in an up and down motion. Edna repeats this several times.

A new shot from Edna's perspective. Her reflective face is on the screen for a brief moment; then the camera follows her gaze to the open balcony door and out to the dark garden below, which looms up like an eerie wilderness.

The preceding shot fades into an interior view of the Pontellier cottage at Grand Isle [Gardner, "Rain Forest"]. In the dawn light we glimpse the crowded disarray. The camera moves somewhat haltingly around the bedroom until it stops on a sleeping Edna; she turns restlessly. As the camera angle shifts to follow its movements, a cat jumps from the bed to the open windowsill and then to the porch rocker, which creaks as the cat jumps off and out of the frame. The camera returns to Edna, who awakens. Offscreen, the distant call of seabirds and the rumble of a delivery cart being pulled along the sandy parkway are heard.

A new shot: looking up to the Lebrun complex, an almost complete view of the hotel and grounds. From this distance we see Edna walking quickly along the gallery to the main house. Reaching the porch, Edna finds the black maid sweeping. She gives her a message to deliver. We, of course, are too far away to hear. While she waits, Edna uncovers the two birdcages, and the birds look at her sleepily. In a moment, Robert appears. He has dressed hurriedly and is still buttoning his blousy silk shirt. As the field of the image narrows to the porch, we see the two converse, and then they walk out of the frame to the left.

The camera makes a quick cut to Robert and Edna in front of the open window of the small kitchen building. They face each other, their upper bodies border the frame's sides. Two large mugs of steaming coffee sit on the ledge between them. The cook hands out a plate of steaming rolls. The two breakfast and engage in an animated conversation.

ROBERT: (Mock scolding) Mrs. Pontellier, you could give a fellow a fair warning. Calixta would have had an early breakfast ready.

EDNA: (Merrily) Wasn't it enough to think of going to the Chênière and waking you up? (They both pause to eat.) Do I have to think of everything, as Léonce says when he's in a bad humor?

The two become silent. In the background people can be heard in the kitchen. Edna wipes crumbs from her mouth with the back of her hand. She drains the cup with a flourish, and then smiles at Robert.

EDNA: Shall we?

The image changes to the wharf. A lugger bobs gently in its mooring. A number of hotel guests have already boarded. As the camera tilts over them, Robert, who is in the boat, reaches up to give Edna a hand as she boards. They sit together on a wooden bench. At the last moment, just as the ropes are being untied, an island woman, MARIE-QUITA, easily climbs aboard. She carries a basket with a gauze cover, under which shrimp wiggle in a mass. Edna looks at her with great interest and the camera moves in close. Mariequita and Robert greet each other in the local patois. Then, both Mariequita and Edna stare at each other with frank interest. Robert, speaking sharply, seems to scold Mariequita.

Now the camera moves back. The field of the image broadens to show waves slapping against the boat and, far beyond, the beautiful horizon dotted with small fir-covered islands. The early morning sun is bright and warm. The camera angle shifts to scan the billowy clouds that move slowly across the sky. Then Edna looks into the direction the breeze carries the boat. She shades her eyes from the sun. After a moment, she turns back toward Grand Isle, and then from her perspective the camera angle reverses to show the receding coastline of the island.

A new shot: from the island wharf of Chênière Caminada. The camera is stationary at the edge of the wharf, facing a short incline. The passengers have disembarked and walk up the hill to a small Gothic church, which is painted brown with yellow trim. As the passengers continue on, the camera pulls back even further; it appears to go right through Edna, who remains alone on the wharf. The camera pans to show the island; it is ancient, with deteriorating yet charming little buildings that dot the landscape in a random pattern. It looks like a miniature. The foliage is a colorful mélange of ripening orange trees, flaming oleander, and decaying oak trees. Then the camera reverses to show the empty wharf and the lugger tied to its mooring.

This last shot dissolves into a sequence that begins with an overall view, from the rear, of the church's interior. The Lebrun guests and several islanders are scattered among the pews. There is a PRIEST at the altar preaching in a barely audible tone. A few phrases are intelligible, such as "the Lord" and "We are His flock." Reverse angle: Edna looks up; something has startled her, and she looks frightened. A quick cut back to the altar. We see what Edna sees—the priest is a different man than in the preceding shot, taller and thinner. He is the man she saw in her beach reverie. It is Edna's father. From the same position, the camera turns to the front pew. There we see a rear view of THREE LITTLE GIRLS, heads bent, who were not there before. The sermon continues in the same manner.

Now the camera shifts to the pews. There is a full shot of Robert as he bends over Edna with an expression of concern. In another pew, M. Farival rises in consternation then awkwardly sits back down.

The image changes: Edna and Robert are in the church's tiny side-yard cemetery. Edna rests on a stone bench and wipes her forehead with a man's large handkerchief. Robert has his foot on the bench; he hovers over her.

EDNA: I don't know what came over me.
ROBERT: It was too hot in there. Who could breathe?
EDNA: I feel better. (She takes off her hat.)
ROBERT: Let me take you to Madame Antoine's. You can rest there.

The next sequence begins during this last line of Robert's. It starts with a series of reverse traveling shots as the camera leads Edna and Robert over a narrow path by the Gulf. There are interposed close shots of the tall reeds in small pools and jagged driftwood fencing. Edna and Robert stop by a well. Robert draws water in a small tin pail to refresh her. They walk on, talking quietly, the camera at too discreet a distance for the audience to hear.

The image changes: the camera shoots toward the interior front of the main room of a primitive little house. Edna bends slightly to enter from a low, rounded door. She looks around her; on one wall of this rustic room is a large fireplace and cooking hearth. To complete the furnishings there is a long, low trunk with an elaborate brass lock and a small table with two rough chairs. Edna steps forward. Robert and MADAME ANTOINE, a large, pleasant looking woman, enter behind her. The three crowd the room. Robert converses with Mme Antoine in patois. Then she nods and studies Edna solicitously. With friendly motions she leads Edna to the open bedroom doorway visible in the left side of the frame.

A new shot: Edna is alone in the tiny bedroom. A large poster bed almost fills the screen. The white coverlet is neatly folded back. An old wood-framed mirror hangs over a small dry sink in a corner. Edna reaches out to clasp the bedpost as the camera moves in close; she is viewed in profile. This image dissolves to a different angle profile shot of Edna, and we notice that she has unpinned her hair. The camera pulls back to a full shot of Edna, in her slip, at the dry sink. The camera is behind her as she bathes her face and arms. Her reflection in the mirror is distorted by its silvering, which is fissured in places.

Now there is a series of shots that, while not dreamlike, have a quality of unreality. Edna first sits on the edge of the bed and bends to remove a stocking. Then she lies precisely in the center of the bed with her arms over the comforter. She raises her arms in a stretching gesture; she studies a bare arm. She runs the other hand lightly up and down its length. She sighs contentedly and rests her arms. Then Edna snuggles down and closes her eyes as she lifts the cover to her neck.

The camera moves unsteadily back to the side and then forward across the bed. It comes to a halt just in front of the little window, whose eight ribbed panes show the side yard indistinctly. Sounds of movement and whispered conversation drift into the room. Then the room becomes a little darker, as though a cloud were passing over the sun. The image changes to a shot of Mme Antoine as she quietly lowers the mosquito net over Edna as she sleeps. Now Edna is alone again; the camera is held for a moment on her sleeping form. Then the camera pans to the window and over to the dry sink and mirror. As the camera pauses there, we notice that the two side panels of this old mirror have been restored; they stand out at an angle. Also, the fissures have disappeared.

The camera turns toward the bed: Edna awakens. Then from her perspective, through the gauze net, the camera slowly pans around the room. Edna notices a folded towel and powder box on the low stool. The camera reverses its path in an exact manner. After a moment, Edna sits up and parts the net.

Now Edna stands at the dry sink and daubs her face with powder. Her motions reflect a mood of contentment. Although the powder is white, her face retains its rosy hue. Edna gazes intently into the mirror, her image reflected in the mirror's three sides.

A new shot: Edna is dressed and is dining alone at Mme Antoine's table. She eats the food that has been left for her—roasted chicken, bread, and wine. After a moment the image changes: from the exterior the camera shoots toward the front of the house [Chopin, Etude in E-Major, Op. 10, No. 3]. Edna emerges from the front door and scans the yard. She shades her eyes from the unaccustomed glare. There is a basket of fruit on the stoop. As Edna sees Robert, who is off to the side, the camera angle changes to encompass both of them in the image. Robert sits under a tree, absorbed in a book. Edna rolls an orange over to him. At first he is startled; then he sees Edna, rises, and comes to her.

EDNA: How long have I slept? It's all so odd. Where is everyone?
ROBERT: You've slept for one hundred years. And I have stood guard.
 (He bows.)

Edna looks at him pensively and walks off to the fence, which is just a few steps past the side of the house. She leans against the stile and Robert follows her. They are both posed in perfect harmony with the stile.

EDNA: Really, Robert, where are the others?
ROBERT: They've left. It was best to let you sleep. I urged them to go on. After all, what was I here for?
EDNA: I wonder if Léonce is worried?
ROBERT: No, he knows you're with me.

Edna leans further back. The pink rays of the setting sun lend a warm glow to the scene. She speaks half-heartedly:

EDNA: Still, we should leave here.
ROBERT: Are you afraid of the pirates' ghosts whispering between the reeds?

EDNA: (She shrugs.) I've never thought of them.

During this last line the image changes to a shot of Edna and Robert preparing a sailboat for departure. It is just before total darkness. Mme Antoine stands on the small pier with a large lantern. The camera pulls back to the middle distance as the boat begins its glide through the marshy channel. Mme Antoine waves a cheerful good-bye and calls "Safe trip!" in her heavily accented English. The camera moves in to track the boat as Robert skillfully oars a path through the twisting bayou. Their two silhouettes are visible in the dark. The eerie atmosphere of the bayou at night, with its dense foliage of moss-draped tree limbs, gnarled mangrove roots, and deformed cypress knobs, is intensified by the creaks, the brushes, and the quiet smack of water against the boat. A sudden splash in the narrow waterway and the call of a heron are heard.

Then the camera turns so that Edna is eliminated from the frame. Robert, who has a pleasing voice, begins to sing the ballad, "Ah! Si Tu Savais," which has been heard before. After a moment, a woman's accompanying hum is heard offscreen. The camera passes across Edna's still face, and we see, even in the shadows, that it is not she who hums. Then in a soft, contented voice she asks:

EDNA: Do you know we have been together the whole day, Robert?

The background hum becomes stronger than Robert's voice, the melody repeated over and over. The swamp mist slowly rises from the dark water; the narrow passage widens. The camera pulls back to reveal more of the surroundings. The boat glides swiftly now, with an air of lightness, and Edna appears perfectly at ease.

The camera turns and comes close along the boat's length. Then, after a moment the camera angle changes to behind the boat and shoots across the open Gulf. Light clouds race across the moon.

Scene 8. Present time: Spring. Transition.

It is night. The camera is at the top of the Pontellier hall staircase. Edna, dressed in the apparel of the "long night," holds a candle for light as the camera follows her down the staircase. She carefully makes her way in the darkness. In the foyer her image is reflected in the hall mirror. We may notice that the mantel clock is no longer there. The camera follows her out through the vestibule. The image fades.

Scene 9. Past time: Winter. Edna paints the Colonel's portrait.

This series of shots begins with a view of Edna's atelier. No one is there. The room is just as before. Edna's paints and brushes are arranged on the oak table, and there is a sketch set up on the easel. Soon we hear voices from the hall, and the door is pushed open. Edna's father, the Colonel, and Edna enter, as she exclaims in annoyance:

EDNA: You promised not to ask me again.

The Colonel assumes a pose on the stool that accentuates his military bearing. Edna mixes the paints, and then she opens her collar.

THE COLONEL: It's cold in here.
EDNA: (She starts to draw.) I hope you will like this.

Now the camera passes across a section of the floor to the door. Raoul and Etienne have crouched low in the hall and peek inside. The camera changes angle to show that Edna still concentrates on her work but that the Colonel has noticed the boys. So as not to disturb his pose, he makes a "kicking" motion with his foot in the direction of the door. With loud shushes the two boys scamper off.

It becomes quiet in the atelier. The camera draws a little closer to Edna as she paints. Her attitude is assured, and her use of the brush is deft. Now the image changes to a shot of the sun as it streams through one of the tall narrow windows. Then the camera returns to Edna. The Colonel's portrait is further developed; the depiction of his posture is much more relaxed than his actual pose. In a moment Edna speaks:

EDNA: What time is it?
THE COLONEL: (Studies his pocket watch) Ten to noon.

EDNA: We said we would attend the races today.
THE COLONEL: Looking forward to it, my dear.

The image changes to a shot of Edna and the Colonel as they start down the staircase. The Colonel is in the rear.

THE COLONEL: What will I tell Janet?
EDNA: Another wedding! I don't really care to see one.
THE COLONEL: Indeed! What a thing for a married woman to say!

Having heard the noise on the stairway, the boys run up to join their mother and grandfather. Edna continues downstairs, but the Colonel stops where he is. The boys are at his side. Etienne sits on a step and peers down as Edna descends. When she reaches the bottom the camera reverses. Now the Colonel turns and goes back upstairs, with the boys in close attendance.

A new shot: the Colonel and the boys are in the atelier. The Colonel stands off to admire the painting. The boys examine the paint jars. Then the camera turns so that just the sketch is in the field of the image.

THE COLONEL: (Offscreen) Well, I dare say, boys, your mother is a very talented woman.

The camera turns to the worktable. We hear the footsteps of the three as they leave the room. Out in the hall the Colonel says:

THE COLONEL: (Offscreen) I'd better see to my gray coat.

Scene 10. Past time: Summer. Edna muses over Robert's sudden announcement; her thoughts go further.

Now there is a sequence of two settings that alternate in a steady, even pace. The first is the bedroom of the Pontellier cottage, and the second is the Lebrun dining hall. We begin with Edna alone in the bedroom. The room is lit for evening but conveys a dreamlike aura. Edna reaches into the closet and takes out a peignoir. Immediately loud voices are heard offscreen and the scene changes.

The animated conversation emanates from the dining hall where dinner is being served. Around the long table are Mme Lebrun,

Victor, Robert, Adèle, Mlle Reisz, M. Farival, the widow, and one or
two other guests. There are several empty places. A maid serves the
soup course. Edna walks into the frame and takes the seat next to
Adèle and across from Robert. The camera is stationary and at a
slight tilt over the scene.

MME LEBRUN: Mrs. Pontellier, Robert has decided to leave us. He's
going to Mexico—
M. FARIVAL: —You are far too lenient with these boys of yours. Taking
off for Mexico!

Edna, soup spoon in hand, interrupts and looks confusedly
around the table.

EDNA: Mexico? At a moment's notice?
ROBERT: I said all along I was going to Mexico.

The camera returns to Edna in the bedroom. She has changed
into the peignoir. She stands still and somewhat distractedly ties the
ribbon belt. Edna looks as though she hasn't decided what to do
next. She rubs her wrist where the dress cuff left a pinch mark. Then
Edna starts to hang up her dress, which is draped over the back of a
chair, but she changes her mind and lets it fall back. This image
dissolves into the dining hall scene, where M. Farival speaks as if
there had been no interruption.

M. FARIVAL: If you don't mind my saying—
ROBERT: (He looks at Edna.) I've been planning to go for years.
EDNA: (She signals the maid.) Tonight.
ADÈLE: This very evening.
M. FARIVAL: What possesses him?

The camera returns to the bedroom. Edna unpins and brushes
her hair in front of the mirror for a moment. Then she goes through
the inner doorway and down the narrow corridor of the cottage to
the children's bedroom. The camera is close behind her. Raoul and
Etienne are in bed. The light is still on, and the nurse stands by.
Edna bends down to kiss Raoul.

RAOUL: A story, Mama.
ETIENNE: Tell us about—

EDNA: (She goes to Etienne.) Not tonight, my sweets. It is already very late.

ETIENNE: But I was waiting for it.

EDNA: (She has walked to the doorway.) Tomorrow I will tell you the story about Grandpa's farm. From beginning to end.

The shot fades and we are returned to the dining hall. Dinner is still being served. The conversation continues as before; everyone talks at once, and over the din, Mme Lebrun calls:

MME LEBRUN: Please . . . Let Robert explain. (She bangs the table with her spoon.) Give him a chance to speak. He has been invited to join a business expedition with our good friend, Monsieur—

VICTOR: (With irritation) Let Robert tell it.

ROBERT: There's nothing to go on about. If I am to meet Monsieur Montel in time to catch the steamer, I must leave tonight.

ADÈLE: I hope you will be cautious, Robert. We Creoles are far too trusting. The Mexicans are friendly, but crafty, no?

MLLE REISZ: They have no music to speak of.

ADÈLE: There is a Mexican cook on Distance Street. Alphonse often stops there. He makes the most delicious—

VICTOR: Make up your mind, Madame Ratignolle, is—

M. FARIVAL: This is too much!

EDNA: (She looks at Robert.) But you said nothing to me.

ADÈLE: When do you leave, Robert?

ROBERT: At ten. Baudelet wants to wait for the moon.

As Robert speaks the last line, the camera returns to Edna's bedroom. She sits by the open window. Idly she picks up the fan and holds it in her lap. There is a soft knock on the open inner door (the beaded drape hangs loose). Robert enters with an air of hesitation.

ROBERT: Aren't you feeling well?

EDNA: Oh, well enough.

Robert sits down on a little chair. He faces Edna from across the small room, his back to the screen.

ROBERT: It should be cooling off by now.

Edna offers him her fan, and he declines it with a small gesture.

ROBERT: It doesn't help. When you stop fanning, the hot air feels all the more uncomfortable.

Edna has been using the fan more vigorously as Robert speaks the preceding dialogue.

EDNA: How like a man to say that! It's ridiculous. (It is quiet for a long moment.)

ROBERT: Must we part in ill humor?

The image changes. Now Edna is alone in the room. She walks about with a distracted look. After a moment, Edna speaks in a voice-over:

EDNA: Can't you understand? I've grown used to seeing you—to our excursions—the old fort—

Now the dialogue continues onscreen as Edna pauses by the screen door.

EDNA: It is so very quiet tonight.

Scene 11. Past time: Summer. Raoul and Etienne, an episode.

The camera follows Raoul and Etienne from a far distance as they playfully run along the shore. Now it is seen that they run toward a spot on the sand where gulls have gathered. In the background the sounds of bathers are heard. Then, as the two boys come closer to the gulls, the sounds fade away until it is quiet. There is a quick close cut to the boys, frontal perspective, as they continue to run. The image shifts to the gulls as they take flight in a startled formation; it is a very close shot. One gull seems to batter the camera. The camera returns to the boys as they come to a sudden halt as the last gull whirs away. Etienne thrusts out his arm to hold Raoul back, the camera pulls away. Both boys look down with a revolted expression. A half-eaten carcass of a large fish lies on the sand. The image changes to a shot of the boys from the rear as they nonchalantly run back to join the others. Etienne has his arms extended in birdlike mimicry.

Scene 12. Present time: Spring. The long night ends; morning comes.

Edna sits up on the settee in the parlor of the "little house." She looks a bit more disheveled than she did in the previous scene of the "long night." It is barely dawn. A white cat rubs himself against her skirt. Edna's motions convey her weariness; she adjusts her dress and smooths her hair. After a moment, she sighs and stands up. The camera shoots from the side as she goes to the little dining room buffet and helps herself to some food on the shelf. She pours a drink from a carafe and slices a piece of cheese. She stands there and eats in a mechanical way. She is lost in thought, as in the earlier scene on the settee, but now there is an edge of resolution to her expression. Edna finishes her meal, and as the camera angle shifts she walks out of the frame.

ACT III

Scene 1. Past time: Léonce consults Dr. Mandelet.

This scene begins with an interior view of the closed lower half of a Dutch door, which we have seen previously. Léonce's dark-suited arm reaches over to unlatch the hook. As it does so, Léonce's voice is heard offscreen.

LÉONCE: I'll let myself in, Doctor.

The shot changes: Dr. Mandelet swivels away from his desk as Léonce enters the study.

LÉONCE: It's Edna that I've come to see you about.
DR. MANDELET: Madame Pontellier, not well? This is a surprise. She seemed positively radiant, when was it?—ah, at the—

The camera is now positioned over Léonce's shoulder toward the doctor. Behind Dr. Mandelet is the window, which looks into the garden. It has a cool-weather appearance; however, there are still some blooms along the neat rows. Léonce interrupts, but Dr. Mandelet listens intently.

LÉONCE: (Offscreen) Ratignolle's. Yes, she seems quite well. But to tell you the truth, I'm at a loss. (Pause) She's acting strangely.

At this disclosure Dr. Mandelet runs his fingers lightly through his beard. Léonce continues to explain Edna's behavior.

LÉONCE: I hardly know where to begin. For one thing, she's let the house go to the dickens.

The camera draws closer to the window view, out of which can be seen a woman, MADAME MANDELET, at work in the garden. With cutting basket and shears, she very deliberately selects flowers for a bouquet. The camera focuses on her while the two men continue their conversation offscreen.

DR. MANDELET: Women are not all alike, my dear boy. We've got to consider—
LÉONCE: (He interrupts again.) Believe me, this goes much further. Her attitude has changed. And toward me. (Pause) You understand.

For a moment the two men are silent. Then Léonce speaks and his voice betrays his irritation.

LÉONCE: She goes strolling about in the streets. She's not herself. I tell you, I don't like it.
DR. MANDELET: Nothing hereditary, is there?

At these words, the camera angle changes to show both men. Dr. Mandelet toys with a pen. Léonce leans back in the chair with an agitated thrust.

LÉONCE: Certainly not. The family is of sound old Kentucky Presbyterian stock.
DR. MANDELET: Why then, send her for a visit. It will do her a world of good.
LÉONCE: That's just it. The youngest sister is getting married soon, and Edna refuses to go. She insists on staying away!

The camera pulls back as Dr. Mandelet rises and goes to a wall cabinet in the background of the frame. He removes a decanter and two glasses, then pours a sherry for himself and Léonce. Each man takes a sip.

DR. MANDELET: (He stays by the cabinet.) Perhaps, Léonce, you should let your wife alone for a time. (Pause) Woman, my dear friend, is a very peculiar and delicate organism.

LÉONCE: But I don't bother her now. And the boys are at my mother's. She takes a delight in showing them the country pleasures of my own boyhood.

DR. MANDELET: (Long pause) Why don't I pay Madame Pontellier a call?

The camera moves to a slightly different angle, as Léonce rises, walks to the door, and looks out. He then turns back into the study, hesitates, and says:

LÉONCE: One more thing. I have to go to New York on business for a few weeks. Edna refuses to come. She puts me off with excuses about her painting. Painting! I (He steps outside.) tell you (Pause), it's devilishly uncomfortable.

The image changes. Now Dr. Mandelet stands at Léonce's diagonal by the half-open door. His hands are in his pockets.

DR. MANDELET: Surely, this is a passing whim of hers. We doctors are familiar with these cases. Give it time, Léonce, give it time.

Now the doctor is alone on the screen [Antonín Dvořák, Symphony No. 9 (Largo)]. He stands in profile with a serious expression, as Léonce's steps resound on the brick walk and then fade away.

Scene 2. Present time: Spring. The journey—another facet.

A new shot: Edna waits in front of a commercial carriage on a French Quarter street. She wears a pale yellow gown and carries her gloves. A yellow velvet rose is attached to her small lavender cloche. It is very early morning, after the "long night." There are only one or two other people about. The camera is stationary, and at a distance,

as Edna lifts her skirt to enter the carriage. Now there are two suc-
cessive cuts: one to Edna's ankle, the other to a man across the street
who stares at her. She pauses to return his gaze and then quickly
boards the carriage. The next shot ends with a slow fade. We see the
carriage's jerky move forward and through the rear window, Edna,
as she steadies herself against the seat. The driver calls, "Suzette,
Tante Suzette," and the heavy wheels clack loudly as the carriage
leaves the screen.

Scene 3. Past time: Winter. Edna at the fairgrounds.

This scene begins with a high traveling movement of the camera,
punctuated by sharp turns, in exploration of a wooded park. The
path of the camera discloses the formal design of a manicured landscape with its varied horticulture and, in particular, its intricate byways. Among the park's aspects we notice the dense foliage of one
area, the mottled sunlight on another, a bee that lingers over a flowering bush, the sky glimpsed through tall trees, and a squirrel's dash
across a gravel path. This shot will continue for a long moment,
while the camera lingers on each perspective.

Then there is a cut to a close shot of a horse in a stall, and the
sound of his impatient trample. A groom, unseen except for his arm
and bent head, brushes the animal's long neck. Offscreen, the loud
and rough voices of several men are heard. Then someone whistles.

This image changes to a close shot of a waiter dressed in a formal
white uniform. On the screen his gloved hands arrange tea and
pastries on a cart. In the immediate background a white rail and part
of a large fern become clear in the image.

The shot changes abruptly. From the air, as though in a balloon on
a wavering course, the camera reveals the large acreage of the fairgrounds. This panoramic impression is of woods that surround
a developed area that consists of a central promenade space, surrounded by the track, two grandstands, an open-air restaurant,
horse barns, and a carriage parking area. There is a lake in the distance. The camera descends with the effect of a rush, but it still
hovers above the scene. The field of the image becomes the promenade area. The crowd that gathers there is predominantly male.

There is an air of gaiety and elegance: a mélange of velvet, crepe, parasols, tall fedoras, canes, and racing sheets. Greatly amplifying this scene are sounds that include an unseen horn band [Mortimer Wilson, "New Orleans"], greetings between friends, and the inevitable hawkers' calls. Shouts of "Candie tire," "Calas," and "La bière" are heard above the din of the crowd and the music.

Now the camera focuses on a couple, gradually seeking them out. They are Edna and her father, arm in arm in the crowd. They look well together: Edna has an animated demeanor, and the Colonel, as before, has a pronounced military bearing.

The image changes to a shot of Edna and her father seated at a wrought-iron table. A fringed umbrella in an Oriental pattern provides shade. The white-gloved waiter of the earlier shot pours coffee at their table. Then several people walk into the frame in extreme closeup, which obscures the image of Edna and the Colonel.

FIRST ACQUAINTANCE: (Offscreen) It's Mrs. Pontellier.

The camera pulls back to reveal TWO WOMEN and a MAN who have stopped by the table. Both women are nondescript. The man is darkly handsome, with the style of a bon vivant.

EDNA: Hello. I waved to you before intermission. (The Colonel rises.) Allow me to present my father, Colonel—
SECOND ACQUAINTANCE: (She interrupts.) Indeed, Sir. It's an honor.
THE COLONEL: The honor is mine, madame.
FIRST ACQUAINTANCE: And this is my good friend, Monsieur Alcée Arobin.

The two women make way as Alcée steps forward between them. He bows to the Colonel, while he stares at Edna.

EDNA: We've met before, haven't we?
ALCÉE: You are quite correct, Madame Pontellier. An unforgettable evening. It was at Les Keifergée. I much admired your costume.
THE COLONEL: I've heard of these balls.
ALCÉE: But now, on seeing you again, I realize that it's your beauty—
THE COLONEL: Did you ladies attend?
ALCÉE: —that engraved the indelible impression.

The two acquaintances titter; the Colonel does not quite know how to react, and Edna appears indifferent. At this moment, a loud bell is rung, and everyone begins to move. The image shifts to Edna, who stays seated. The Colonel is heard offscreen:

THE COLONEL: Edna?
EDNA: I'm coming.

A new shot: the group of five starts back to the grandstands. The camera follows close behind through the crowd. Edna and Alcée are in the rear, and in front, the two acquaintances are on each side of the Colonel. He gives each woman an arm to clasp.

FIRST ACQUAINTANCE: Would you favor us with a tip for the next race?
THE COLONEL: I defer to my daughter. (Oratorically) Several generations of devotion to the finest of Kentucky horseflesh is her legacy—
EDNA: Father, please!
THE COLONEL: —and the added ingredient, inherited from her mother, God rest her soul, the luck of the Irish!

The Colonel's speech is met with laughter, which fades away as the shot dissolves into an image of the three women together in the ladies' grandstand. Immediately an exaggerated sound of horses thundering around the track is heard. The camera draws closer to Edna as she trains her binoculars on the track. In the lens we glimpse a reflection of the race. Then the camera turns to the track. This series of shots should convey the power and excitement of a horse race. We see closeup fragments of jockeys and horses and hear heavy breathing as well as thundering hooves. In the background bettors shout their encouragement. Reverse angle: Edna puts the binoculars aside and watches intently. Then reverse to the race again, but to a close shot of one particular horse, who recklessly presses forward.

Now there is a quick cut to an empty stall in the horse barn, and the sound fades. Next is a new image of the two grandstands from the middle distance. It is between races, and there is a subdued hum of activity and conversation. The camera moves in closer and locates Edna as she gazes toward the men's grandstand. The angle reverses: Alcée waves in her direction. Next to him is the Colonel.

A new shot: the Colonel assists Edna into the Pontellier carriage. The two acquaintances and Alcée stand by, and then Alcée moves forward and puts his hand on the rein as the Colonel climbs aboard. Alcée looks up to Edna and speaks to her in a teasing manner:

ALCÉE: You are certainly at home here. I'd like to be here again when you are. Possibly I could pay off my debts for the entire season.
EDNA: (She smiles.) I am not always so lucky.
FIRST ACQUAINTANCE: We've missed you, Edna.
SECOND ACQUAINTANCE: Why not dine with us?

The Colonel takes the reins and replies for himself and Edna.

THE COLONEL: We accept with pleasure. But first you must promise to let me mix a cocktail of my own invention!

Scene 4. Present time: Spring. Boarding the train.

This next series of shots will almost have the look of a different film. The interior of the train station is ugly, with a dingy and stifling atmosphere. The camera slowly rotates. Overall there is both a smokiness and a glaring light, the most artificial yet. The people are in dark travel clothes. The next shot is from inside the ticket office. The camera shoots from in back of the clerk through the divider bars, and toward Edna, who bends slightly to arrange her ticket. Her face is impassive. We become aware of the station noises, which include an indistinct clamor in several languages, the competitive calls of the vendors, and the sounds of the trains themselves.

There is a dissolve to a closeup of a section of an engine. Smoke billows across the screen. The camera slides away to focus on Edna as she boards the third car. A conductor leans down to help her. He says something, to which she shakes her head "no" as he assists her up into the train. The image changes to Edna walking down a narrow corridor. There are very few passengers in the compartments. Slowly the train pulls out of the station. Edna peers through the window of an empty compartment; then she goes inside. The train moves faster. Through the windowed door across to the other side of the compartment we see the New Orleans levee in a whir of blurred images.

Scene 5. Reverie: Summer's end.

A new shot: the screen is divided between sea and beach. A beautiful summer sky of pale blue, floating clouds, and blazing sun presents a leisurely aura. In the middle distance Edna cavorts in the shallows with Raoul and Etienne. There are only a few others on the shore. We hear the sounds of the sea and the playful shouts of the two boys. With an affectionate gesture, Edna waves them to shore. At first they protest, but Edna insists. At the water's edge the nurse waits with their robes folded in her arms. Ill-humoredly the two little boys dawdle to shore.

The camera comes closer to Edna as she gracefully turns and trails her fingers in the surf. Edna walks to a deeper spot and plunges forward. She swims steadily in the center of the frame for a long moment before the shot fades.

The camera begins a lateral movement across the shore to the bathhouses, then to the path, where Mlle Reisz stands at its entrance. She stares out to sea. Then Edna enters the frame from the left. She wears a daygown, her face is flushed, and her hair is damp. She looks happy.

MLLE REISZ: Here comes our beautiful sea creature.
EDNA: Hello.
MLLE REISZ: You've the knack well, Madame Pontellier.

The two face each other, turn, and enter the path together.

EDNA: Thank you, Madame. It is my one pleasure.

In a reverse traveling shot, from a further distance than the previous journeys along the path, the camera leads as the two wend their slow way back to the hotel. They are congenial together. Mademoiselle offers Edna a chocolate from her sack.

MLLE REISZ: Do you miss your friend?
EDNA: Yes. Don't we all?
MLLE REISZ: He is the only Lebrun worth troubling about. I've known Robert since he was a boy. He used to find his way to my poor studio.
EDNA: Robert?

MLLE REISZ: Of course! He's not one to forget an old woman. And you, madame, will you come to see me in the city?
EDNA: I will surprise you. (Long pause) When do you leave?
MLLE REISZ: Next Monday. And you?

The shot changes. Both women are in front of Mlle Reisz's cottage. Edna stands with a foot on the bottom step and her hand on the newel post while the musician climbs the steps to the porch.

EDNA: It has been a pleasant summer, hasn't it, mademoiselle?

Scene 6. Past time: Winter. Edna and Léonce at dinner.

A new shot: of the interior vestibule door of the Pontellier house from the hall. It is evening, and the house is well illuminated. Through the frosted and clear glass foliage design of the door, we glimpse Léonce as he removes his outer garments in the vestibule. When Léonce enters the foyer the camera moves to a side position to reveal the wide expanse of hall and stairway. He pauses at the sideboard table to examine the calling cards in a silver tray. Next he looks at himself in the gilt mirror above the table and straightens his tie. Léonce's attention is caught by a reflected object; this is a small bronzed statue of a boy reading under a tree. Then there is a closeup of the statue. Léonce turns and looks around the room. His eyes take in several objects of decor; among them are waxed flowers in an oval frame, a glass beaded drapery pull, and a table clock that is placed on the end of the sideboard. The clock is of white glazed china with scenes of Paris painted on the case. The camera moves closer to the clock until Léonce leaves the screen; then Léonce's hand appears in the frame and lightly rests on the case.

The image changes to the parlor. This room has many of the flourishes of an upper-class formal room of New Orleans in the Victorian era, yet it is undistinguished. There is a small rococo desk and a pedestal table with ornate legs next to an easy chair of large proportions. Between several other chairs of various styles is an étagère that holds a collection of Oriental objects. Edna is at the desk, with notepaper and writing implements placed before her. She is dressed informally in a negligee. Léonce enters through double wooden doors. He gives her a light kiss and squeezes her shoulder as he says:

LÉONCE: Am I late?

He goes to the easy chair and unfolds the newspaper, becoming absorbed by the front page.

LÉONCE: The mayor will have this town booming again. Tired out, Edna?

From upstairs come the muffled sounds of children at play. Edna continues to write. Léonce speaks again, but he keeps his eyes on the paper.

LÉONCE: Whom did you have? Many of the ladies?

During the last phrase the camera moves in closer to Léonce. Edna's shadow is visible on the carpet.

EDNA: (Offscreen) I was out today.

Just then a maid appears in the connecting door to the dining room. The Pontelliers rise and silently go in to dinner. The room is furnished with heavy dark mahogany pieces. The table is luxuriously set for two. The camera is stationary at a distance to the length of the table. Léonce seats Edna at one end and takes his seat at the other. The soup course has already been served. The couple simultaneously take up their spoons. The maid has disappeared.

LÉONCE: You were saying, Edna? (Pause) Many of the ladies?
EDNA: I don't know, Léonce. I went out.
LÉONCE: Out, my dear. What urgent business took you out on your reception day?

During this last sentence Léonce adds seasonings to the soup.

EDNA: I went for a walk. (Long pause) I enjoyed it. Did you know th—
LÉONCE: Well, I hope you left some suitable excuse.
EDNA: I asked Joe to say that I was not at home.
LÉONCE: Not at home? (He puts his spoon down.) Edna, we've got to

observe the formalities. To keep up. (Looks down at his plate.) This soup is really impossible. (Pause) Was Mrs. Belthrop here?

Edna jumps up; she is visibly disturbed. Then there is a quick cut to Edna as she walks back into the dining room and places the silver tray in front of Léonce. She seats herself with a flourish as Léonce stares. After a moment, he picks up a card. Edna looks calmer. Now a new shot is superimposed over the barely discernible forms of Edna and Léonce. It is of TWO YOUNG WOMEN at the Pontellier front door. They wear large bonnets. Joe opens the door, and they each hand him a card. At the same time that we see this shot, Léonce's voice is heard.

LÉONCE: The Misses Delasidas. Nice girls. Time they were getting married.

Now the superimposition fades out. The dining room scene is as it was. Léonce selects another card from the tray. He maintains an air of normality. As Léonce continues to speak, the maid removes the soup plates and tidies Léonce's place.

LÉONCE: Mrs. Belthrop. (Pause) I'll tell you what it is, Edna. We can't afford to snub the Belthrops. His business is worth a good round sum to me. Enough to pay for a half-dozen Paris gowns.

Léonce selects still another card and continues to speak. Edna eats heartily. The camera rotates evenly between them.

LÉONCE: Madame Laforce. Came all the way from Carrollton. Poor old soul.

The maid is busy at the buffet with covered dishes. She will mechanically serve the main course dishes during this next exchange of dialogue between Léonce and Edna.

EDNA: Mercy! One time in six years. Just once. And you treat it so seriously.
LÉONCE: It may seem trifling to you, but people don't do such things. Not if they expect to get ahead.

Edna picks at her food, while Léonce takes a bite and then puts his fork down with distaste.

LÉONCE: We spend enough money in this house to expect at least one decent meal a day.

EDNA: You used to think the cook was a treasure.

LÉONCE: It needs looking after, my dear. (He rises.) My wife at the helm.

EDNA: Where are you going?

LÉONCE: My club.

This scene dissolves into a shot of the dining room from another perspective [Gardner, "Mooncircles"]. The room is darker, but with a warm glow of candlelight. The camera focuses on Edna as she enjoys her dessert. The maid appears.

MAID: Coffee in here, madame?

EDNA: Yes. Yes, please. Tell Cook the tart was delicious.

Edna puts her fork down. She turns her head to the camera with a subtle flicker of a smile on her face as the shot fades.

Scene 7. Present time: Spring. On the way to the Gulf.

Edna looks out the window of her train compartment. In the left foreground of the screen we see her profile, with particular attention to her hand, as it rests lightly on the window. The ride seems smooth. The rural landscape rolls by. What we see from the long window is the Louisiana marshlands, with their grasses turned brown by cool weather. In the background a graceful silvery band of bayous traces its narrow curving way to the sea. This shot is held for a long moment. It is an unchanging panorama that contrasts the desolate, barren flatland with the loveliness of the bayous.

Scene 8. Reverie: Winter. A walk and a visit.

This will be a long sequence. It begins with Edna on a solitary walk through the streets of the French Quarter's commercial district. The first shot is of a tiled street sign embedded in the sidewalk and a section of Edna's skirt at the edge of the screen [Guiraud, "Sylvia"].

She wears a long gray woolen cape. The day is overcast and chilly. The camera angle reverses to reveal Edna as she looks downward at the sign. Now the shot changes. The camera will follow Edna on a steady trajectory through these streets, never losing sight of her as the shots change in alternation with fragmented perspectives, distance shots, and frames of Edna that also concentrate on her immediate surroundings. This series will communicate Edna's aimless path in contrast with her secure demeanor. The streets are old and shabby, with sudden byways into arcades and side streets that are little more than alleys. Second-story apartments and offices all have ironwork balconies supported by posts to the sidewalk. These provide an overhang for pedestrians, as well as a shadowy aspect. The streets are crowded with people of every description: businessmen, dockworkers, servants on errands, and other indigenous inhabitants. There is a profusion of vendors in stalls, with portable carts, or with rustic boxes filled with wares. These include the flower vendors, the praline sellers, the syrup-ice seller, the palmetto-root-broom man, and the rice-cake stall. It quickly becomes clear that Edna is the only unescorted white woman in this business and market district. The little streetcars lurch in the road, and bicyclists hug the curb to avoid the cumbersome carriages. Edna weaves her way through the scene as a deliberate and curious observer. She is a stranger, but nevertheless comfortable in this milieu.

At one point Edna will pause in front of a candy shop, La Confiserie de Boule. The camera will remain stationary during this scene at an angle that allows visibility through the window into the shop. Edna peers through the multipaned window at display shelves crowded with colorful boxes. She goes inside, where she converses with the shopkeeper. Through the window we observe her selection of two boxes, each with a toy painted on the lid, and a larger box with a papier-mâché rose on the cover. Edna writes a note and then leaves the shop without the purchases.

On the street again she continues her walk. There will be a cut to another street here [Gottschalk, "La Bamboula"]. Edna stops in front of a corner store; concealing the interior are bizarre-looking paintings on the window. The designs consist of convoluted patterns of abstract and voodoo symbols in deep colors of red, purple, and black. Edna remains for a moment in front of the store before she approaches the beaded curtain door. Just as she does so, a hand brushes the curtain aside, startling her. Now the camera is just behind Edna as she studies the interior. Inside are sparsely stocked shelves of small jars, burning candles, signs in French, and strange objects on sharp hooks. These include twisted rope balls and feathered masks. There is an impression of empty space. Almost like an apparition, the PROPRIETOR rises from her chair and comes forward. Her tignon is piled to an incredible height. The elderly black woman beckons to Edna with a smile. Reverse angle to Edna: her face is impassive, but she backs away. The curtain, held open by an invisible someone, swings closed. In the vestibule a white man waits for Edna to leave. His face is shadowed.

Quickly, unthinkingly, Edna changes her mind and parts the curtain to enter the store. The proprietor is waiting for her. She faces the camera, Edna has her back to the camera.

EDNA: I am only passing by.
PROPRIETOR: Madame has lost her wedding ring.
EDNA: Why, no. How could I?
PROPRIETOR: You must decide—

She takes Edna's hand and lifts it. Her ring finger is bare. Suddenly we notice the candles, arranged around the altar carelessly, flickering in the shadows.

PROPRIETOR: Ah, I see. I am mistaken.
EDNA: I will come again.

Immediately the shot changes to an image of Edna as she boards a streetcar. This sequence will move quickly. The shot changes to inside the car, where the camera follows Edna as she selects a seat that is removed from the other passengers. She looks out the window. Then the camera cuts to an exterior shot of Edna; her cape almost fills the screen as she descends from the car. The car moves away in front of her, momentarily obscuring her from view. We then see her as she waits on the corner as though unsure of her direction. This appears to be an old residential neighborhood. Edna decides and walks out of the frame.

The next shot is a fade-in to Edna in front of a door in an uppermost landing of small dimensions and dark corners. Edna almost fills the space. From inside the door Mlle Reisz calls out:

MLLE REISZ: Entrez!

Edna shyly opens the door and steps inside the apartment. The camera is stationary and at an angle that shows the room's entire dimensions. The apartment is small, sparsely furnished, and shabby, but interesting. In addition to the piano, which dominates, there are other signs of Mademoiselle's profession, such as a music stand and stacks of sheet music. There is a quaint sofa, a very old black-walnut cabinet with faded ornamentation in the Oriental style, and two curtainless dormer windows.

At the sight of Edna, Mlle Reisz jumps up from her desk, scattering her composition sheets.

MLLE REISZ: So! You remembered me at last.

Edna is drawn into the room. She hands Mademoiselle a sack.

EDNA: To remind you of our summer teas.

Mlle Reisz peeks into the bag, and her eyes light up as she withdraws one of the small pastries. She replaces it and sets the sack on the tea table as Edna removes her cape, hat, and gloves. They both settle themselves on the sofa.

MLLE REISZ: And how is la belle dame? Always handsome, always healthy, always contented.
EDNA: Well, you presume. (Pause) I'm studying painting. As I used to.
MLLE REISZ: Always the sketch pad!
EDNA: I'm becoming an artist.
MLLE REISZ: An artist! Indeed. You aim high, Mrs. Pontellier.
EDNA: Well, what do you think of it?
MLLE REISZ: Do I know you well enough to say?
EDNA: You must.
MLLE REISZ: An artist's life . . . (She shakes her head.)

The image changes. The two are still on the sofa, only now there are the effects of a coffee service on the table. Edna, cup in hand, leans back against the pillows.

EDNA: Will you play for me, Mademoiselle?

Silently, the musician puts her cup down and goes to the piano. She begins an étude [Chopin, C-Sharp Minor, Op. 10, No. 4]. The music seems to fill and then move beyond the confines of the apartment. Edna goes to the window and leans against the wall. She looks out and then moves forward enough to look down. Immediately, and from her perspective, the camera travels down to the small courtyard several stories below. It is enclosed by a high brick wall with ironwork trim. Two little girls, seen earlier in church and in Edna's reverie, are having a tea at a child-sized table-and-chair set. They pour and sip from their toy china in perfect mimicry of adults. The music floats down from above.

Now the image returns to the apartment. Edna still leans against the wall. The music becomes softer, but no less insistent.

EDNA: I'm going to move out of my house.
MLLE REISZ: Ah.
EDNA: Aren't you astonished?
MLLE REISZ: What does Mr. Pontellier think?
EDNA: What is there to say? Léonce has business in New York. The
    boys are with their grandmother in the country.

The camera remains stationary as Edna begins to walk around the room restlessly.

EDNA: Just two steps away. (Pause) Think of it!

As Edna becomes more excited the camera angle changes to emphasize the narrow dimensions of the room. Edna paces and says:

EDNA: This little house is around the corner from us. It always looks
    so inviting, so restful. Only this morning, as I was passing by, I
    noticed it's for rent.

Edna stops by the window again. As she looks out, there is a quick cut, hardly long enough to be sure, of the courtyard, which is now empty. There is only the grass and a few flowers. Edna's energy has become dissipated. She continues to speak, but with a flat tone.

EDNA: I'm simply tired of looking after that big house. It's never seemed like mine, (Pause) like home. Too many servants, too much bother. I'm tired. I'm tired of it all.

For a moment, there is just the music as Mademoiselle plays on. Then she speaks, but without looking at Edna, who is behind her.

MLLE REISZ: That's not your true reason, ma belle.

Edna sits on the sofa. She seems weary.

MLLE REISZ: You needn't confide in me.
EDNA: The house, the money that provides for it, they aren't mine. Isn't that reason enough?
MLLE REISZ: (She stops and turns to Edna.) They are your husband's?
EDNA: Yes. It's a whim of mine. There is a little money from my mother's estate. Sent to me in small payments. (She smiles; the music stops.) I've been lucky at the races. But more importantly I've sold several of my sketches. The dealer says the work grows in force and individuality. (Long pause) I cannot judge of that myself.

Edna looks questioningly at Mademoiselle, who joins her on the sofa.

MLLE REISZ: Ah, the artistic soul—
EDNA: (Clasping her hands) Oh, Mademoiselle, I know I will like it.
MLLE REISZ: —that dares and defies.
EDNA: (With a push against the pillows) Léonce will think I'm demented. But for once, I want to be myself. Perhaps I can make him understand.
MLLE REISZ: And who is this by my side? Is it really my dear Edna?
EDNA: (With a smile) I've been asking just that question.

The two sit together in a companionable silence for a moment. Edna helps herself to a pastry from the sack. She seems revived.

EDNA: I'm going to give a grand dinner before I leave the old house. We'll have everything that you like. We'll eat and drink. We'll sing, and laugh, and be merry for once.

The image changes: the two women stand by the open doorway.

EDNA AND MLLE REISZ: (In unison) Au revoir.

As Edna closes the door behind her, Mademoiselle speaks to herself. Dusk is visible through the windows.

MLLE REISZ: It grows late.

Scene 9. Present time: Spring. Edna boards a steamer.

A new shot: from a distant and high perspective the camera looks down on the scene of a small port's wharf. There is very little activity. In the middle of one of the piers, Edna stands immobile. In the background, a steamer, the *Ada*, is being loaded with a commercial cargo. Around her there is an atmosphere of the fishing industry—nets hang to dry and huge wicker baskets hold fish arranged in careful layers. There are no other passengers. As the camera slides in closer, the captain turns a corner of the *Ada*'s upper deck. He waves to Edna. She looks up and then walks forward to the ship's side. Edna walks up the boarding plank, and no one stops to assist her. As Edna passes from pier to ship we notice a compact sign posted on the wharf. It lists a half-dozen island destinations, one of which is Grand Isle.

Scene 10. Past time: Winter. Adèle visits Edna in the "little house."

A new shot: this is the street in front of Edna's "little house." The day is sunny, with the softness of a southern winter just before spring. Adèle walks into the frame. She has the awkward gait of the last stage of pregnancy. Adèle pauses and looks around her. The image changes to a shot of her as she timidly pushes a gate open. There, in the courtyard, is Edna, busy with a study of a dozing cat.

ADÈLE: So, I have found you!

The cat runs off as Edna jumps up. The two friends embrace, then stand off from each other, hands enclasped.

EDNA: Adèle! I never thought you'd leave home now.
ADÈLE: Mon dieu! It was a sudden urge.

EDNA: (She playfully swings Adèle's arms.) Come, let's sit in the sun.
ADÈLE: I wanted so to see your little house.

Edna tenderly leads her to the front stoop. They both sit there, Edna on a higher step. Adèle continues:

ADÈLE: I came by Fidelia Street. There isn't a soul there this time of day. But now I am exhausted. And Alphonse will scold.
EDNA: (She strokes Adèle's cheek.) But I'm so glad to see you. I've thought of you so often lately.
ADÈLE: And I you, Chérie. (Pause) Now tell me, what's this we hear about the Pontelliers? Renovations and a trip to the Continent. I had no idea.
EDNA: (Quite serious now, her hands folded in her lap.) Ah, that's just Léonce's way of explaining me to the world.
ADÈLE: Léonce is right, Edna. People do talk.
EDNA: He's angry with me. And I do miss him. It's unkind. Alone in a strange place.
ADÈLE: But, tell me, do you like living here, Edna?
EDNA: (She rises, then with a teasing air.) Let's have a tisane. Celestine's brew is marvelous. It will restore you, as Alphonse Ratignolle would say.

The last sentence is heard offscreen as the image changes to the two women on the settee in Edna's parlor. The camera is at a high tilt. During this conversation they will have tea.

EDNA: I'm content here. I come and go as I please. I'm just getting used to it.
ADÈLE: Will you go home?
EDNA: This is becoming my home. I've the comfort of my own—
ADÈLE: Edna, is all this wise? I've come here to tell you, as your friend, to be careful.
EDNA: Yes?
ADÈLE: How can I say it?
EDNA: You may say whatever you wish to me.
ADÈLE: Well, then, Alcée Arobin has a dreadful reputation.
EDNA: He means nothing to me.

Edna rises and goes to the settee. She stretches out there as the shot changes, so that the camera faces the settee lengthwise.

EDNA: At times his company is pleasant.
ADÈLE: (Offscreen) Mme Lebrun paid us a visit. She speaks the same
of Victor. And she has news from Robert. He is on his way home.

It's difficult to gauge Edna's reaction to this news. Her face reveals
her pleasure, yet she speaks with an edge of irritation.

EDNA: I didn't hear a word. (Pause) Why did he forget about me?
ADÈLE: (Offscreen) Robert? Forget you! Perhaps, Edna, he feared to
remember you.
EDNA: Then, do you thi—

The camera pulls back as Adèle rises.

ADÈLE: I'm becoming uneasy. When will I see you again?
EDNA: (She rises.) Let me order the carriage. You've overdone.
ADÈLE: (She fusses with her dress.) Yes. I cannot refuse.

A new shot: Edna and Adèle stand by the front gate, Edna inside,
and Adèle outside. They are at an angle to each other.

ADÈLE: Will you be with me, when my time comes? You are so calm.
EDNA: Of course, Adèle. Send for me. I will come at once.
ADÈLE: Promise?
EDNA: Whatever time of day or night.

Scene 11. Past time: Winter. Edna gives a dinner party.

A new shot: slowly and with a lateral movement the camera pulls
back to unfold the full glamor of the Pontellier dining room transformed into a luxuriant setting. The heavy draperies of the background wall are drawn to reveal the opulent side garden; the glass
French doors stand open. Elegant lamps illuminate the thick foliage.
Standing alone in the center is a small fountain, with water gently
cascading down its three tiers. The dining room is rearranged for the
dinner party. The table is lengthwise in the frame, with the garden
for a background. The table looks sumptuous; there are silver and
gold table settings, damask linen, yellow silk shades over miniature
candles, and at each place a small bouquet of the ever-present roses.

Around the table upholstered chairs of every description add to the *Arabian Nights* mood.

A narrow aspect of Edna's figure appears at the edge of the frame. Reverse angle: Edna surveys the scene before her. Her satin ball gown is in harmony with the decor of the room. A lace shawl flutters from her bare shoulders to the pale gold dress. The only sound is the quiet fall of the fountain's flow.

Now the shot changes to Edna at the front door where she admits Alphonse.

ALPHONSE: My apologies, Edna. We thought it best that Madame Ratignolle conserve her strength.

EDNA: Come quickly, Alphonse. Let's not waste a moment of this lovely evening.

The image returns to the dining room. All the other guests have already arrived and are seated. The camera remains at a sufficient distance, so that the greetings are observed more than they are heard. Edna ushers Alphonse to his seat. The other guests are Mlle Reisz, Victor and Mme Lebrun, Alcée Arobin, the first acquaintance of the fairgrounds scene and her HUSBAND, and TWO OTHER MEMBERS of Edna's circle. The camera moves closer until the dimensions of the dining room border the screen. Soft strains of a guitar are heard. This is the same melody that Victor played the night of the swimming party and that Robert sang as he and Edna sailed home.

MME LEBRUN: Something new, Edna?

A quick cut to Edna that focuses on her tiara of brilliant gems, set rather majestically on her head.

EDNA: Quite new. Brand new, in fact. A present from Léonce. I may as well admit that this is my birthday.

As the camera pulls back to the exact position of the preceding shot, a chorus of felicitations is heard from around the table. Because all speak at once, only a word or phrase is heard distinctly, such as "Bon anniversaire," "Santé," and "À tes amours." At this moment, two maids appear with silver trays laden with dishes. This image dissolves into a shadowy glimpse of the interior of the "little house." Again, the image dissolves into a close shot of the garden fountain.

Then, suddenly, a closeup of Edna. The sounds of the dinner are heard as a muffled din. Now the image of Edna's face fades into a shot of her full figure as she stands alone by the fountain. Her hand rests lightly on the oval bowl of a tier; water plays over her fingers. Then there is a close shot of the carved stone pineapple at the fountain's center.

The sounds of voices and of the guitar fade away. Alcée joins Edna in the image; he stands on the other side of the fountain. Alcée seems uncertain, while Edna is still and reflective.

ALCÉE: Well?
EDNA: Well.
ALCÉE: What now?
EDNA: All that remains is to lock up the house.

A new shot: Edna and Alcée at the front door as he turns the key in the lock. It is now very dark, with deep shadows. He takes Edna by the arm and leads her from the veranda to the sidewalk. Her shimmering gown is the one focal point of this image. The camera follows them around to the side. It is a short walk to the "little house." The shot changes to one of Edna, and she opens the front door. Alcée stands in back of her. Through a window the light of a table lamp shines brightly. Edna half turns back to Alcée, as he strokes her shoulder.

EDNA: I thought you were going.
ALCÉE: I am, after I've said good night.
EDNA: (She doesn't move.) Good night.

Edna turns, with a hesitant gesture, and steps into the house. She closes the door behind her. Alcée remains on the porch.

The image changes to Edna inside the house. She puts down her beaded purse and removes the tiara.

EDNA: I left my camellia.

She looks around her with an absent-minded air. Idly she looks at her easel. The sketch is of tall stalks of grain.

EDNA: No matter.

Scene 12. Reverie: Winter's end. Edna seeks the café.

A new shot: the camera is stationary; it looks across and down a street in an unfashionable residential area. The quality of this afternoon's light has an unusual luminosity; it diffuses a warm glow over the scene. Ivy climbs over cracked brick walls; ironwork fences and balconies have a moldering look. Still, it is a charming vista. Edna walks into the frame from the background corner. She wears a pale blue gown of a gauzy fabric; it has a summery appearance. Suddenly there is a loud whir of wings and the call of sea gulls. Startled, Edna looks up to the sky. A quick cut to follow her gaze, but there is nothing there, just the sky. And the sound of the birds quickly fades away. Edna looks puzzled.

She continues to walk up the street, and the camera moves back as she approaches. Then Edna stops in front of a very high gate, whose loose hinges effect a tilt. She confidently pushes it open, and it is quite clear that Edna has been here before.

The image changes to her perspective of the intimate retreat beyond the gate. A wall of the old stone house fills the background; checkered curtains border the small windows; and flowering plants are arranged on the brick ledges. In the courtyard several tables are artfully placed between or under orange trees. Remnants of food are left on one table, and its chairs are awry. The effect is of age, and of coziness, and even of an undisturbed sanctuary.

Edna moves forward; her figure obscures the courtyard for a brief instant. Then the image changes to a shot of Edna comfortably ensconced at a table, her book open in front of her. It is even more obvious now just how lovely the courtyard is. Patterns of sun filtered through leafy branches shelter Edna, and the soft chirps of birds as they flitter about a tree feeder are clearly heard. For a moment the camera slides away to linger on these tiny birds, and a soft breeze ruffles the leaves of the tree. Then the camera moves back to a position that discloses the greater part of the courtyard. A BLACK WOMAN, confident and comely, steps out from the open door of the house with a beverage basket. She hands Edna a tall glass of milk and greets her.

PROPRIETOR: Bonjour, madame. Returned? So soon?

EDNA: Why not? When you treat me so well. And at this moment,
I'm perfectly famished. It's a long walk from Esplanade Street.
PROPRIETOR: Bien! All afternoon a hen roasts. Epatant, eh?
EDNA: Perfect.

The proprietor smiles with animation and walks deliberately back into the house. This shot dissolves and is followed by a shot of Edna, still at the table. The book is closed, and there are the remains of a meal in front of her. She holds a coffee cup to her lips with both hands, as she slowly savors its taste.

Reverse angle: to Robert as he enters from the gate. The camera slides away to the middle distance. Both Edna and Robert are astonished. Edna rises in clumsy haste.

EDNA: Why, Robert, is it really you?

He hurries forward and takes both her hands in his, then in a simultaneous movement, they both sit down.

ROBERT: Edna. (Pause) I had no idea you knew this place.
EDNA: You're back, Robert. But when did you return?
ROBERT: Now that I'm with you—
EDNA: (She lets go of his hands.) You didn't even write to me.
ROBERT: (He leans back.) I didn't think my letters would interest
you.
EDNA: That's not true, Robert. We're never ourselves. It tires me to
think of it.
ROBERT: I thought of it.

While Edna speaks Robert reaches back and with his pocketknife clips a rose from the low bush against the house. Until this moment it had not been noticeable. The image shifts, and the camera draws closer until there is only the rose in Robert's hand, Edna's face, and the immediate background. Edna's expression softens into contentment.

EDNA: Come home with me. I want you to see my place.

The camera pulls back and the field of the image becomes the two at the table.

ROBERT: My mother told me you've moved. I thought you would

have gone to New York with Mr. Pontellier, or to Iberville with the children.

EDNA: Will you come?

ROBERT: You know I want to.

This image dissolves into a shot of Edna and Robert as they enter the door to the "little house." The camera is inside at an angle toward the door.

EDNA: I want to hear about everything you did in Mexico.

Now there is a quick cut to a shot of both of them on the settee, at a facing angle to each other. The afternoon light has softened into dusk.

ROBERT: It's the same everywhere. I'd much rather hear about you. How have you occupied yourself, Mrs. Pontellier?

EDNA: (This is said like poetry as she looks offscreen.) I've been seeing the waves and the white beach of Grand Isle; the quiet, grassy street of the Chênière; I've been working like a machine and feeling like a lost soul. There was nothing interesting. (Pause) And you, Robert?

In the silence that follows these lines, Robert gives Edna a quizzical look. He is about to say something, then changes his mind. Just then a knock at the door startles them. Edna looks as though she expects to hear bad news. When she answers the door, there is a little child, who hands her a note. Edna reads silently and then speaks, her face turned to the door.

EDNA: It's Adèle. I must go at once.

ROBERT: (He rises.) Let me go with you.

EDNA: (As she puts her hat on) Stay, Robert. Stay here and wait for me.

ROBERT: Edna! Don't leave . . . Please.

Robert has come to the doorway and stands there with Edna. She places her hand gently on his arm, then hurries out (the child waits). Edna pauses as the camera draws closer to her.

EDNA: I'll return as soon as I can. I will find you here.

Scene 13. Present time: Spring. Arrival at Grand Isle.

The camera rounds a corner of the parkway that leads to the Lebrun Hotel. The sounds of a hammer are heard. The image changes to a shot of a corner of the porch, where Victor is at work on the repair of a plank. With him is Mariequita. She sits on the floor with her legs crossed under her. The camera moves back as Edna walks into the frame from the right foreground. Now the camera angle reverses to Edna. She looks tired and a bit disordered.

EDNA: Hello. I walked up from the wharf. I heard the noise. (She comes a few steps closer.) I guessed it was you mending the porch. (She looks around.) How dreary and deserted everything looks.

Reverse angle: to Victor and Mariequita, who now stand on the edge of the porch, Mariequita slightly behind Victor. They look as though they see a ghost.

VICTOR: Mrs. Pontellier! (Astonished) But, you didn't send word.
EDNA: There wasn't time.
VICTOR: Nothing is fixed up yet.
EDNA: Any corner will do.

It is silent for a moment; Victor comes down the steps.

VICTOR: I've lost my manners. Come, you will want to rest and freshen up.
EDNA: (She turns to the lawn and shades her eyes in a familiar gesture.) Thank you, Victor. But, first, I have a notion to go down to the beach for a walk. (Pause) Even a swim. (She hands Victor her hat.)
VICTOR AND MARIEQUITA: (In unison) It's too cold!
VICTOR: Don't think of it.
EDNA: (As she walks away and calls back) Why, it seems to me that the sun is hot enough.

The camera reverses to Victor, who stands there with a puzzled expression.

VICTOR: She might have sent word.

A new shot: the interior of a bathhouse, with some light admitted through the partially opened door. Edna is in her slip. She removes her jewelry in an unthinking way. As she places her double locket on a small ledge, it falls open. The image cuts to its miniature portraits; they are of Raoul and Etienne.

The image changes to Edna in her bathing costume as she walks along the shore. We hear the sound of the waves. She appears to be reflective and content, yet with an edge, as though she needs to absorb all the richness of sea, shore, and sky. During this long sequence the camera stays at a steady distance in front of Edna; it seems to lead her along. There is a cut to Edna's feet as she burrows her toes in the warm sand. Then, as the scene progresses, and almost imperceptibly, the camera moves closer. All of a sudden, just as in the scene in front of the café, we hear the whir and call of sea gulls. They sound extremely close. Edna looks up with joy as the camera cuts to the sky above her. But there is nothing there, and it has become quiet again, except for the subtle sound of the sea. Now Edna stands still. The camera moves downward to her feet, where small eddies of the sea reach her. The camera remains there, and in a moment, Edna's suit falls to the sand, and she steps out of it. She takes several steps, just into the edge of the water. The camera pulls back and up to the middle distance, to reveal her, nude, from the rear. She is poised on the edge of the sea [Gardner, "Winter Night, Gibbous Moon"].

The image changes to the sea, which fills the screen. In the center of the frame Edna swims forward, with strong rhythmic strokes. The camera comes in very close; there is just Edna and the rolling waves that splash against her as she parts the water with flagging strokes. Then Edna lifts her face. She looks frightened, as though a bad memory has overtaken her. Edna regains her impassive expression, swims on, falters; her breath comes in winded gasps. Exhausted, she swims forward as the field of the image widens some. The tumult of the sea becomes more apparent on the screen. The camera dips to a lower angle, to a point where our view of Edna is lost in the depth of a wave. Then, as before, we see the sea from a slightly further distance. There is only the sea. This is held for a long moment before fading.

Scene 14. Present time: Epilogue. Adèle reads aloud.

A new shot: Adèle rests comfortably in bed. An open book lies on the coverlet. It is afternoon. The camera is in the middle distance and stationary for this shot. The bedroom door is ajar. Brisk footsteps are heard, and then Alphonse peeks in. He comes forward to Adèle's bedside. Beside her, the new baby rests comfortably in her wicker cradle.

ALPHONSE: Reading, my sweet? Don't tire yourself.

Alphonse bends over her, and Adèle picks up the book.

ADÈLE: "There was the hum of bees,—"

As Adèle speaks the last line there are two cuts, one to the counter of the pale marble dry sink, the other to the open window.

ADÈLE: "—and the musky odor of pinks filled the air."

The End

INTERPRETATION

The true woman is as yet a dream of the future.
Elizabeth Cady Stanton
International Council of Women address, 1888

She felt like some new-born creature, opening its eyes in a
familiar world that it had never known before.
Kate Chopin, *The Awakening*

Edna Pontellier is one of the more compelling and enduring characters in U.S. fiction. She exerts an individuality and charismatic strength so powerful that modern readers claim her as an icon, identifying Edna as a timeless symbol of women's quest. As her name implies, Chopin's heroine is truly a "bridgemaker." This idea represents the core of this study: the conversion of Chopin's literary character to a cinematic character of equal complexity, wherein Edna's interior journey of revelation and rebirth is presented in such a way that the authenticity of Chopin's theme and era is retained as the modern appeal of Edna's quest is reconceptualized in filmic terms. The various formal aspects of this interpretation of the screenplay—structure, characterization, setting, soundtrack, for example—radiate outward in this discussion as spokes of a central focus, which is, of course, Edna.

One of the more intriguing and persistent theoretical issues in adaptation studies contrasts the facility of fiction to portray the inner self with words to film's more imprecise language of images. Decades ago Sergei Eisenstein compared the dialectical thought processes of the mind with synthesizing opposing elements in film images. The cinematic dialectic gives film its creative energy and sense, he claimed, as a technical mirroring of the human thought process. In Robbe-Grillet's well-known phrase, "The mind is the province of cinema." With more particularity James Belson's study illustrates how extrinsic and intrinsic characterization, landscape and frame montage, the close-up and the dream, all achieve an inner life on the screen. The art of representing the interiority resembles montage: "A method of organizing material on the principle of laconicism, juxtaposing pieces of the outer world in 'part-whole thinking,' [reveals] the psyche through its relationship with the physical."[1] The rendering of the dream, the close-up, landscape, and dualities are all innate to *The Awakening*. Edna, who conjures up mental scenes to convey her thoughts, ideas, and insights, is visually oriented. Thought and sensory and visual perception make up consciousness, which the avant-gardist Kate Chopin understood.

Chopin liked to say that she wrote quickly, with little revision, taking advantage of ideas as they formed. Yet, the structure of *The Awakening* is so complex that reflections on whether her prose is the result of "unconscious selection" as claimed or the creation of a precise design are overshadowed by appreciation of its originality and significance. One pervasive thematic device, dialectical patterns, presents an interesting example. Among Chopin scholars George Arms first noted this tendency, the "constant contrasts" emanating from the dual life, "the author's way of looking at life." Jane Tompkins suggests that the novel is built on a bipolar axis, with the narrator creating a duality "in the world before her, by the alternation of lyric and satiric moods."[2]

The novel sets up an intricate set of oppositions at every turn of the narrative. Edna announces this as a philosophical juxtaposition: "[to] comprehend the significance of life, that monster made up of beauty and brutality" (*CW*, 967). In the screenplay Chopin's narrative device is converted by development of a series of alternating images and ideas that illustrates the form of the conflict within Edna as she seeks to resolve woman's struggle between the questioning self and the formidable restrictions of culture. While there are numerous dialectical aspects to Chopin's novel, at the center is Edna, an embodiment of duality. A woman of "contradictory impulses," Edna "apprehended instinctively the dual life," and as Chopin tells us, even her physical appearance "has a contradictory subtle play of features" (*CW*, 883).

For the Edna of the screenplay I portray these dualities as a dialogue between Chopin and her character on "women's lot," with Adèle Ratignolle and Mlle Reisz each enacting a facet of the more extreme experiences and yearnings of author and protagonist. This is not to say that *The Awakening* is an autobiographical novel. It does contain Chopin's most vigorous and daring discourse on the subjugation of women and examines questions that Chopin pondered deeply for several decades and then, as a mature woman of forty-eight and a successful author, felt confident enough to express. Victorian inequities preoccupied Chopin, and her own life offered opportunity for profound reflection on gender repression in the pull between conformity and freedom. Many scholars read the novel as a "balanced act of the imagination" that leads the reader to the discovery of the inauthenticity of Victorian myths of gender.[3] That Chopin, a woman of intellectual depth and intuitive knowing, experienced the conflicts her heroine suffers is the genesis for the novel's most intriguing contrast: the creative dialogue between author and protagonist.

For example, the idea of time as an element of women's biological principles, culture, imagination, and quest is woven into the structure of the screenplay. It is a focus of the dialectical impulses that Edna and Chopin experience, and as an organizational device elaborates the screenplay's themes. Time becomes a blueprint for the internal rhythms of a life dramatically altered by the quest for female autonomy. Compatible with Chopin's own narrative sequences through which Edna wanders in her "mazes of inward contemplation," the scenes are structured as a cyclical journey through a labyrinth. Cyclical time is also associated with Chopin's use of the intuitive as a natural and nonsequential mode of knowing, which celebrates female wisdom. In *The Awakening* time is rarely mentioned: "Time doesn't concern me," Edna answers, when Mlle Reisz cautions her that the hour has grown late as the two friends spend a pleasant afternoon together.

Chopin's use of women's time frame involves both natural and cultural concepts. The lives of her characters, taken from experience, are based on unvarying daily rituals that do not depend on clock time. The endless routine of domestic life and the trivial occupations of their leisure convey a purposelessness through the small and undirected events of the day. Even the women's physical attitudes, their languorous poses and delicate gestures, deepen the sense of timelessness in the novel. The scenes of the screenplay are intended to simulate natural fluctuations of mood heightened by biological cycles to induce moods of calm, vigor, despondency, and exhilaration. These scenes are timed to emphasize Edna's impatience with restrictive and trite tasks, as well as with the affectations of culturally endowed femininity. Rather than chronology, it is feeling that endows time with form. Edna's situation evolves from moods, memories, solitary thought, and instinctual revelations to reveal women's inner world and development.

The first critic to notice the "peculiar timeless quality" of *The Awakening* is Emily Toth, who found little differentiation between seasons, no references to dates, and time of day rarely mentioned except by Léonce, who represents traditional masculinity. Toth notes that the absence of time complements Chopin's lyrical and epiphanic mode: "[F]emale experiences of time are actually closer to the daily world all people experience—in that our lives are not purposeful progressions, but significant moments." Robbe-Grillet makes a similar point in an explanation of the unconventional time chronology in *Last Year at Marienbad:* "Mental time, with its peculiarities, its gaps, its obsessions, its obscure areas, is the one that interests us since it is the tempo of our emotions, of our life."[4]

Contemporary women filmmakers have used the tenseless image to convey the pain of women ensnared by social codes. Often cited for its innovative chronology is Chantal Akerman's *Jeanne Dielman, 23 Quai du Commerce—1080 Bruxelles* (1975). Akerman's scenes explore the banalities of Jeanne's life by faithful observation of her routine. The film's structure carefully balances the sadness we must feel for a squandered life with the dignity accorded Jeanne's effort to survive within a limited scope. This kind of representation of immediacy is useful to convey Edna's situation.

There is also, beyond the mysteries of seasonal and clock time in *The Awakening,* a cycle of female experience that marks gestation to birth, and more subtly, to rebirth. The novel encompasses two pregnancies, one real, one symbolic. The actual duration of the novel is the nine months of Adèle's pregnancy; each scene in which she appears has some mention of her condition. We are meant to see the development of Adèle's pregnancy as an ironic parallel to Edna's gradual inner growth, which culminates in her ultimate awakening.

Edna's metaphysical gestation, which begins as a moment of "stirring—she knew not what," grows to her ultimate symbolic regeneration in the sea and is contrasted with Adèle's pregnancy. In a subtle opposition of traditional expectations Edna becomes more vital and alive as she casts off custom for experience, while Adèle becomes less capable and withdraws from participation in active life as her pregnancy advances. Adèle's condition is viewed as an illness; she is "incapacitated," the narrator remarks. Dr. Mandelet, on the other hand, notices that Edna is "palpitant with the forces of life." This reversal of ideology is an amusing example of how Chopin plays with the Victorian reverence for motherhood as she contrasts the experiences of Adèle and Edna. This irony is underscored in the screenplay.

In act 1 only the birth sequences occur in the present, and they provide a link to the other scenes, which take place in the mind. In acts 2 and 3 only Edna's final journey is enacted in the present. The one exception is the epilogue, which brings the development back to the birth scene, where Adèle's infant offers a connection between Edna's lack of resolution and the hope of continuation of the female quest into the future.

This shifting back and forth in time and space connects the ideas of the screenplay to the vague and mystical forces of the novel. Edna weighs events of the past and present, and even predicts the future. Time becomes an important structural device that governs Edna's growth and marks the progression of events as they may have occurred in the mind, seemingly without order. The sequences illustrate the organic intellectual and intuitive development of Edna.

The dialectic operates on many levels. Edna's actions move between abstraction and embodiment, between limitation and freedom. This ambiguity removes events from linear time and leads to a more enigmatic and impressionistic time frame. In his study of *The Awakening* Robert Arner finds this ambiguity a "dislocation of spatial and temporal boundaries which stimulate mental processes." Arner points out that time ceases to be measurable in units: "This alternate suspension and enjambment of time functions thematically in the end both to indicate the centrality of Edna's experiences and to point backwards to the 'beginning of things.' "[5] Our sense of time is suspended while Edna is in the spell of the sun's rays; when she is in the sea, time moves swiftly. Edna has the time, because she has no sustained occupation, to immerse herself in nature, to think and later to awaken. Chopin, in an autobiographical reference, spoke of emerging "from the vast solitude" about the time before she became an author.

Impressionistic time is associated with another Chopin symbol that is closely interwoven with the use of time in the adaptation, Edna's dream-doze state. Chopin was fascinated with the dream state as a way to unravel thought. In several of her short stories hypnosis and the drug-induced dream are extensions of the dream-doze mode. Indeed, they are often the only alternatives available to a woman because more overt action is impossible. The dream state, Chopin suggests, is a traditional form of feminine behavior. In "Elizabeth Strock's One Story" the protagonist "walked about days in a kind of a dream, turning and twisting things in my mind just like I often saw old ladies twisting quilt patches around to compose a design" (CW, 586–87). In The Awakening Edna "sleepwalks" through her dreamy days with time in suspension. She lies in the hammock, not because she is tired—she is not—as she tells Robert, but rather to dream and to "feel like one who gradually awakes out of a dream" (CW, 913). She dozes over Emerson not because she is bored or incapable of intellectual thought, as some critics have suggested, but because as Virginia Kouidis remarks, "Emerson shapes and reflects the sexual chauvinism against which women have had to defend and define themselves."[6] In a state of somnolence Edna experiences the "realities pressing into her soul" (CW, 912). She is on a quest to solve the puzzle of patriarchal order and, in so doing, to attain the true Edna.

The urgency of Edna's journey unfolds through time and space. Shifts between scenes in the imagination are accomplished with natural movements and effects, such as a cloud of road dust filling the screen in a prolonged silent moment, or Edna's curved arm sweeping across the image in a graceful arc to reveal another scene. These scenes are structured with a rhythmic spirallike effect to evoke "scenes of the mind," a technique that recalls Chopin's narrative. For example, when Edna meets Mlle Reisz on the beach the two engage in conversation, and Edna "thinks of" scenes she relives in her imagination. Mlle Riesz "echo[es]," as Edna says, "the feeling which constantly possessed her" (CW, 927). This effect is reinforced in the screenplay with reverie. Real incidents of life are sifted through layers of memory and thought until truth is blurred by time. There are only moments in which the sea is clear; the haze lifts, and impressions emerge.

The "impressions" that Edna, foregrounded in nature, experiences as intuition and reason are directly linked to impressionism as a movement in visual art. In her fiction and essays Chopin alluded to impressionism to illustrate the tenuousness and relativity of experience. In her review of Zola's *Lourdes,* she makes an analogy between a Monet painting and the novel: "Truth rests upon a shifting base and is apt to be kaleidoscopic" (*CW,* 697). Chopin admired impressionism's psychological possibilities. Of her own writing style, she said it was "the spontaneous expression of impressions gathered" (*CW,* 722). "Impressions," both as Chopin experienced her art and as a conduit of meaning in *The Awakening,* provide the source of the screenplay's visual style.

As a literary convention impressionism conveys a style through which intuitive and fleeting "impressions" become a metaphor for the respect with which Chopin seeks to endow Edna's selection of felt "truths." In a paraphrase of a standard definition of impressionism Chopin says that Edna "was seeing with different eyes and making the acquaintance of new conditions in herself that colored and changed her environment" (*CW,* 921). When Chopin, for example, sketches a scene in the tiny café courtyard in which "the checkered sunlight filtered through the quivering leaves overhead" (*CW,* 989), the reader anticipates a change in Edna.

Cyrille Arnavon, in 1946, was the first to notice that Chopin's impressionistic style connects truth and vision in her work. Since then, other critics have developed this point: "The way scenes, mood, action, and character are fused reminds one not so much of literature as of an impressionistic painting." Carol Merrill suggests the novel may be read as a diagram of states of light that indicate Edna's experience, and "the color reflections in the water reflect her state of mind." The shifting shadows and modulated colors illustrate Edna's reveries as she "changes her vision back and forth in time much as an impressionist might paint fluctuating spatial relationships with color." Chopin reflects Edna's gaze in water, windows, and mirrors to evoke psychological penetration. Commenting on the "almost impressionistic improvisation" of the first chapter, Sandra Gilbert calls it an overture, after which "as one scene dissolves into another [the mise-en-scène becomes as] vividly literal as objects in a painting by Renoir or Seurat." Gilbert concludes, "Here, therefore, every object and figure has not only a literal domestic function and a dreamlike symbolic radiance but a distinctly female symbolic significance."[7]

Impressionism as a motif of the Victorian age depicts a "world transposed into exquisite arrangements which reveal the surprising shapes embedded in the everyday milieu." Chopin's novel presents diminutive panoramas—lush beach scenes peopled with opulently dressed women and austere men, "befurbelowed" children playing croquet under spreading trees, and family groups arranged at abundant tables. These vignettes seem to evoke the subjects and the style of the impressionist painters. The tone of Chopin's painterly scenes, the shimmer of sun, the changing hues, the complex portraits—all have a spatial dimension that brings to mind light, air, and texture. As Michael Gilmore notes, she "flecks her pages with vivid dabs of paint."[8]

Arner points out that the "impressionistic technique employed in *The Awakening* intensifies the quality of sensory experience as a means of transcending the purely physical, and of creating a world elsewhere, a world poised between fact and imagination."[9] This stylistic technique creates a sense of the subconscious insights Edna experiences as she moves toward awareness. As her insights surface, her vision clears.

In an interesting interpretation of Chopin's novel Gilmore draws on a less commented on but intriguing aspect of impressionism as a critique of conventional values through its unregulated vision: "Where Edna and the Impressionists most agree, then, is in their common turning inward, their transfer of allegiance from the outer world to the personality and freedom of the individual." Gilmore finds impressionism an "aesthetic analogue" to Edna's unconventional journey.[10]

Similarly Griselda Pollock's study of Mary Cassatt connects the artist's impressionism to female authenticity: "Woman as spectacle gave way to woman in private mental activity." Cassatt's work was both "feminine in its fidelity to the social realities of a middle-class woman and thoroughly feminist in the way it questioned, transformed, and subverted the traditional images of Woman, Madonna, Venus, Vanity, and Eve, in accordance with the aspirations of women to be *someone* and not *something.*" Pollock maintains that Cassatt's many portraits of women reading illustrate their involvement in serious intellectual pursuit rather than idle amusement: "The radical implications of self-absorption and sustained activity in portrayals of middle-class women cannot be sufficiently emphasized."[11]

Because it has taken almost a century to interpret the distinctions of a feminist impressionism, I assume that Chopin presents Edna in her "contemplative poses" without the appearance of "excessive femininity" through intuitive insight. In the screenplay Edna's physical bearing mirrors Cassatt's technique: she looks into the camera directly; she is observed in profile, angled and still; or she is framed with a distance between her and the viewer to show respect for her private space. It is important to see Edna's essential womanliness; she is without guile, coyness, or flirtatious ways. Her penetrating gazes into the camera, into a mirror, through a window reflection, highlight Edna's serious pursuit of self. At times, the camera frames Edna in a series of fragmented shots because she is not yet her "whole self." These shots alternate with close shots to emphasize her habit of introspection.

To provide greater clarity to these postures I have given Edna several distinctive gestures, which when repeated suggest her habit of protracted introspection. For example, she will poke a long, stiff finger through her chignon to show her distraction. After I had developed a series of hand gestures for Edna, I read Margit Stange's provocative analysis of Edna's proprietary gestures, such as in reaching out for her rings, her hands then foreshadowing her later resolve "never again to belong to another than herself."[12]

Even Edna's tears are not the conventional sign of a woman's weakness. Her sighs and tears indicate repressed thoughts. Chopin says of Edna, "It moved her to dreams, to thoughtfulness—when she had abandoned herself to tears" (*CW,* 893). I too view Edna's tears as the sign of some inner realization, and in the screenplay they are followed by an image that asserts her individuality. In yet another conversion Chopin's obfuscating imagery of veils, gauzy birdcage drapery, and mosquito netting are contrasted with the sun's rays to imply impressionism's blurred effect and to illustrate Edna's conflict.

In the translation of impressionism from a literary to a cinematic style, I focused on the Louisiana setting to provide an atmosphere that evokes Edna's journey to self-awareness: "The gulf looked far away, melting hazily into the blue of the horizon" (*CW*, 882). The balancing of landscape and state of mind lends pictorial authenticity to the screenplay and serves as an emblem of its diffuse structure. As scenes shift back and forth in time, and Edna "sees the connection now," the structure alternates between moods of light and shadow, mystery and revelation.

I both draw on the epiphanies in the novel and create new analogues to render an impressionistic mode. On the beach with Adèle Edna visualizes the traumatic episode of her mother's funeral service. She sees it as she is now, not as the child she was then. This double vision allows for the revelation that adult comprehension brings to childhood recollections. Later, in the church scene, as a dissolve transforms the priest into Edna's father, she is overcome by the memory.

The screenplay provides other objective signs that reveal Edna's inner self. To illustrate Edna's thoughts, I show clouds moving across the sky. She stands in a doorway framed half in light and half in shadow, just as her own inner illumination is divided by convention and rebellion. Another image of Edna shows her face in focus and her still hands blurred. The ambiguity of complex thought is portrayed by these images. The curtains lifting and fluttering in the night breeze should call to mind the stirring moment Mlle Reisz's music occasioned. With these sounds echoing in her mind, Edna experiences a moment of insight by the shore, and she is brought to further revelation. As the summer slowly passes, Edna becomes increasingly involved with her mental development. In the scene where she joins Adèle on the porch, for example, she is doubly distracted, once from the sewing lesson and then from her book. Neither activity brings the satisfaction Edna derives from her own thoughts. These moments of freedom reveal Edna's entrapment in domesticity and her search for alternatives. They chart Edna's movement from restriction toward autonomy.

Two films served as catalysts for the visual atmosphere I wanted to evoke, although thematically neither relates to *The Awakening*. Both films were made in the Soviet Union in the 1970s, one by a Japanese film company. *A Slave of Love* is about a Russian film company making a film at a beautiful sea resort just as the 1917 revolution is about to begin. There are sun-drenched gardens, hot dusty roads, pale colors, and vivid contours, all lovingly displayed as a series of poses by a camera that moves slowly and penetratingly. There are moments of haunting beauty when a character gazes into the camera to reveal the vulnerability of people caught in a crisis not of their own making. *Dersu Uzala*, the Japanese film, is about friendship in an unforgettable landscape. The camera appears almost to penetrate the leaf-blanketed streams and sunlight filtered through branches, disturbed by oddly disorienting frames of the protagonist's hand intruding on the peaceful image. The sound track projects a natural quietude, which connects us to the protagonist's anxiety. Then, when the hum of bees is heard, the aura of expectation is heightened.

Overall, the atmosphere and tone I sought to capture matches Richard Roud's comment on setting in *The Go-Between:* "You can feel the clothes, you can smell the heat," and these physical details achieve "an almost palpable sense of reality, which gives the moral force of the film a greater intensity."[13] In the screenplay I have drawn on the visual aspects of this technique—view, angles, and colors—to capture Edna's search for autonomy. Beyond these reasons, impressionism expresses beauty and is an appropriate style with which to record the characters and their evanescence in their unique and lush settings.

Setting plays an even more important role in the screenplay than in the novel. As Joan Mellen remarks, the redefinition of women in film will not achieve a new image of woman unless her "values and self-consciousness are placed in relation to ideas she experiences as a member of a particular social class." Such a precise setting offers what both Sylvia Plath and Mellen refer to as a "disturbance in mirrors."[14] Edna's setting reflects with cameralike precision the manner and values of her culture and provides the dialectical structure in which her struggle to achieve authenticity takes place. *The Awakening*'s setting also provides an intriguing background for a cinematic adaptation that illustrates the structure and themes of the novel in terms of the contrasts between nature and civilization as a metaphor for the human condition. Women filmmakers have turned to texture, mood, and setting—milieu, in other words—as a way of telling a woman's story.

The power of place also has a significant interpretive function for women's literature. Annis Pratt argues that, "since women are alienated from time and space, their plots take on cyclical, rather than linear form and their houses and landscapes surreal properties."[15] In *The Awakening,* this outer terrain becomes a metaphor for psychological territory. Setting is portrayed with such intensity and complexity that it takes on the power ordinarily associated with character. It is unyielding and, as a consequence, offers Edna the "disturbance" of an uncompromising reality. Edna's surroundings reflect her inward journey. The screenplay, of course, as an abbreviated form, can only suggest the characteristics of the era.

Louisiana history details the constant merging of people and place. The built environment was as much created by the nature of the people who settled there as the natural environment defined these same people. The geographic isolation of the port city encouraged the development of "provincial traits and manners, [and] has preserved the individuality of the many races that give it color, morals, and character." The era of *The Awakening,* the Gilded Age, was epitomized in the original and rare setting of New Orleans, its environs, and its inhabitants: "The 1880s and 1890s were the years that New Orleans was most genuinely New Orleans." A long list of residents, such as Grace King, and distinguished travelers to the area, such as Mark Twain, wrote about its exotic and foreign charm.[16] The locale seemed to bring out a luxuriant prose noted for the flow of its romantic description. However, the physical and social milieu of Louisiana so perceptively captured by Chopin with a "few swift, deft brush strokes" hardly needs to be embellished to emphasize its unique variance from the typical U.S. landscape and culture.

Few have done a better job in relating the setting's atmosphere and exoticism than New Orleans native Truman Capote: "The prevalence of steep walls, of obscuring foliage, of tall thick locked iron gates, of shuttered windows, of dark tunnels leading to overgrown gardens where mimosa and camellias contrast colors and lazing lizards, flicking their forked tongues, race along palm fronds—all this is not accidental decor, but architecture deliberately concocted to camouflage, to mask." Capote calls New Orleans the most secretive of cities, very unlike the city outsiders are permitted to observe. He attributes the "secretiveness" to the undisturbed continuance of Creole family life.[17]

The contrast between the masculine, open, bustling port life and the cloistered domestic scene of high walls and hidden interiors that fostered women's alienation provides a dramatic juxtaposition of social dynamics. Canal Street, by the river, was the center of the commercial district. As the frontier between two cultures the area was a vivid mix of history, custom, and prejudice: "One feature that amused was the complete demarcation which existed between the French and American population. A street divided the two quarters, and if it had been a wide ocean the dissimilarity could not have been more positive." The wide street was bordered by two- and three-story buildings with "lumbering vehicles, elegant carriages, and a fussy little street railroad, all run[ning] in parallel lines along the wide roadway."[18] Clouds of yellow dust from the levee filtered over all.

A memoir of the era recalls the scene: "To the noise made by the hackmen and Negro boys, should be added the jingling of the mulebells, the rattling of the horse cars, the warning grunt of the locomotive's steam horn, and the rumbling of innumerable drays bearing the rich products of Louisiana to the levee for shipment," all mingled in a "hot and sweet confusion."[19]

Large harbor companies lined the streets; they too had "iron lace" balconies and posts to the streets. On the ground floors specialists sold their wares in little shops, bakeries, apothecaries, coffeehouses, and letter-writing stores: "All the shops had signs that were small and artistic and added to the charm of the street."[20] The levee, a terminus for 150 streets and a wide thoroughfare itself, stood at the end of Canal Street. But the nerve center of Canal Street was the French Market.

The market was a huge rambling building, its roof supported by thick columns and its floor punctuated by hundreds of stalls. Food, goods, and people mingled in a colorful mélange. Choctaw Indian women, their papooses strapped to their backs, squatted in front of reed mats to sell spices. Black women sold candies from large flat wicker baskets draped in cheesecloth. Their elaborate head scarves, the colorful tignons, were a trademark. The men of the Creole families did all of the shopping as it was deemed unseemly for a white woman to be out on the streets. Mingling with sailors, dockhands, businessmen, policemen, and travelers were the Creole aristocrats, boutonnieres in place, trailed by servants with packages of shrimps, turtles, strawberries, roses, and pomegranates.[21] The market in its vast array symbolized the complexities of New Orleans's diverse social structure.

At its height in the commercial districts, a community street style was also found in the residential neighborhoods. The high walls imparted an impression of serenity within; however, this quiet lifestyle was often disturbed by street activity. Food hawkers went door to door calling their wares of ginger cakes, pralines, pineapple, beer, and fried oysters. Milk wagons with enormous pewter cans on the seat lumbered down the streets ringing their bronze bells. Small wagons with glass showcases filled with sewing paraphernalia came by daily, and merchandise vendors walked the streets with tin boxes tied to their backs. At dusk the ice cream wagons with illuminated glass signs attracted the children and their nurses. As night descended on the French Quarter, the last remaining worker, the lamplighter, made his rounds.[22]

But it is the architecture and interiors of these homes that best reflect the rituals and restriction of the Creole lifestyle: "The houses of the *Vieux Carré* are symbols of the character of those who built them." The two-story houses blended both Spanish and French influences. They boasted thick brick and stucco walls, "tunneled *porte-cocheres*," hidden courtyards with gates of thick wooden planks concealing lush gardens, and domed passageways built high enough to accommodate the coachmen's towering beaver hats. The cast-iron trim for which New Orleans is famous came in intricate designs such as the magnolia, bow and arrow, or the "two doves pecking in a bowl of pomegranates" pattern.[23]

Edna's address, Esplanade Street, is a New Orleans boulevard that was known as a prestigious Creole address. Other actual places Chopin mentions are Chartres and Canal streets, and the Jockey Club. A visitor of the era, Lady Duffus Hardy, notes that the "[p]ure white buildings shaded by beautiful magnolias and surrounded by shrubs and flowers form a vista charming to the eye and soothing to the senses."[24] In the novel Chopin conveys the setting with a light touch. In her description of the Pontellier home she captures a particular mood: "It was a large, double cottage, with a broad front veranda, whose round, fluted columns support the sloping roof." She describes the interior, with its "rich and tasteful draperies," and mentions the garden with "flowers and plants of every description which flourish in South Louisiana" (*CW,* 931).

On Esplanade and other French Quarter streets stately mansions contained "huge shadowy apartments" for the several generations of the large families that commonly lived together. Interiors were opulent, featuring spiral staircases with carved handrails, stained-glass fan windows, marble floors, intricate cornices, and lavish furnishings. The heavy ornate furniture was of mahogany and rosewood. Large buffets held china from Sèvres, Chantilly patch boxes, porcelain flowers from Vincennes, and other French treasures. The salons of thick velvet- and satin-upholstered pieces were filled with gilt-framed mirrors, bronze clocks, tasseled pillows, pots of tall ferns, and pale Oriental carpets. A piano held the place of honor. The central feature of the master bedroom was its huge canopied bed with an "accouchement couch" placed at the foot. Every room held vases of flowers, and when roses were in season women carried baskets to friends, and men wore boutonnieres.[25]

French Quarter homes were made for prestige, family enjoyment, and lavish entertainments. Hospitality, a common diversion, was extended to friend and stranger alike. A record of these gatherings is preserved in the letters and journals that survive the era. Jessie Benton Fremont, entertained in one such home at mid-century, wrote about the experience in her memoir. It is worth quoting a lengthy passage because the scene evokes Edna's famous dinner party. The sixteen-course dinner, Fremont wrote, concluded with dessert:

> For the dessert we went into another room, large and lofty and opening wide upon the garden, where the moonlight was making fairy effects on the feathery foliage and changed the spray of the fountains to showering diamond dust. The table was covered with flowers, and all of its service was crystal and gold. The Venetian glass chandelier, with its many wax lights reflected in the prismatic glass, was so wreathed and hung with flowers as to make a subdued charming light on the table, which had on it only fruits and ices and fragrant wines. In a wide circle were young slaves in white, each with a great long-

handled fan of peacocks' feathers which they waved gently . . . large mirrors lined the room and repeated this lovely picture of softly brilliant light on flowers and waving peacock plumes, and made an endless vista of the garden and fountains whose fragrant freshness gave both animation and repose.[26]

Had Chopin cared to give such a complete description, Edna's dinner party would have echoed Mrs. Fremont's reminiscence. In the screenplay I use Fremont's description to create a background for the dinner party scene and to emphasize it as a complex externalization of Edna's dilemma. In the screenplay, as in the novel, these rituals—reception day, family ceremonies, and entertainments—are sketched not so much for their splendor as to dramatize Edna's situation of complexity and doubt.

The novel's most expressive physical counterpoint is the opposition of the bustling city to the tranquil country atmosphere of Grand Isle. The diminutive panorama of Edna on the island resort as Chopin knew it no longer exists. Much of the island's natural beauty and many of its buildings were destroyed in the hurricane of 1893. Yet so masterly are Chopin's narrative skills that the island comes alive. As Seyersted said: "We *see* [emphasis added] the Lebrun pension and the bent oaks, the sandy paths, and the Gulf caressing the beach."[27] As New Orleans set the standard for the romantic in cities, Grand Isle epitomized a romantic natural haven. Chopin created a microcosm of New Orleans's exotic Creole culture on the tiny but vividly complex island.

South of New Orleans, the island, seven and one-half miles long and from one-half to one mile in width, is the setting for many legends of Indians and coastal pirates. The regional people were called Baratarians, after the winding Bayou Barataria that links the marshlands between New Orleans and the islands. A mid-nineteenth-century description by Carolyn Ramsey recalls a primitive land: "From the beach road tiny lanes led into the center of the island. These were lost in the crisscrossing of other, still smaller trails which tunneled their way through lush tropical vegetation to the weather-beaten houses of the Baratarians."[28]

Of the many visitors to the island and its environs, none was more captivated by its "strange lands and seas" than Lafcadio Hearn. The vivid descriptions in his famous story *Chita* (1889) range from the experience of "floating through somber mazes of swamp forest, past assemblages of cypresses all hoary with parasitic tillandsia" to the "dazzling sand and shells" of the beach with its "five stooping silhouettes [oak trees] in line against the horizon, like fleeing women." Hearn concludes: "With its imposing groves of live oak, its golden wreath of orange trees, its odorous lanes of oleander, its broad grazing-meadows yellow-starred with wild camomile, Grand Isle remains the prettiest island of the gulf."[29]

The first developers who arrived on Grand Isle tried to convert the land to sugarcane plantations. After this attempt failed they tried crops of cotton, indigo, citrus, and commercially raised terrapins. Later, Grand Isle found its true business when resorts flourished. After the Civil War, the first hotel entrepreneur, Joseph Krantz, purchased a former plantation and made the slave cabins comfortable for the Creoles, turning the old sugar mill into a dining hall and lounge rooms. Chopin recreates Krantz's hotel as Klein's in *The Awakening*.

The island became a popular summer retreat for Creoles escaping the heat and fear of yellow fever epidemics that haunted the humid city. In contrast to other women who tended to go north, with their children, the family-minded Creoles remained close enough to the city to permit husbands weekend respites. The Chopin family joined in this annual custom, as recalled by a family friend who told Rankin that the "long summer vacation times were spent with the children at Grand Isle."[30]

Orrick Johns, a journalist and the son of a friend of Chopin, poignantly recalls the atmosphere of the island in his 1911 memoirs: "The swaying rows of Chinese lanterns on the lawn, the flurry of white dresses, the perfume of women and wildflowers—all the strange beauty of that time, which to everybody remains like a fairy-dream unmatched by later experience."[31] In a short story, "A Family Affair," Chopin describes this scene: "the Chinese lanterns all festooned among the oaks, with three musicians from the quarters playing the fiddle, the guitar, and accordion on the gallery" (*CW*, 582).

By relying on nature, Chopin achieves a powerful and poignant setting for her themes. From the inland waterways to the open sea, from the burning sun to the shady paths, the Grand Isle setting evokes a recurring parallel to the alterations that enclose, echo, and explain Edna's inner search. The cultural setting is equally denotative. Surrounded by sea and sky, the guests at Madame Lebrun's stand out in cohesive yet ambiguous unity. Both the isolation and the pastoral surroundings accentuate the Creoles' dependency on their culture as a natural and eternal verity. But that is a naive myth, for underneath the calm sky dissent brews, however oblique it may be. To suggest the complex social community Sandra Gilbert locates another of the novel's sly oppositions. The Lebrun resort seems to be a "woman's colony," owned by a woman and principally inhabited by women and children (except for weekends), where they are free to express themselves and learn from each other as contrasted with their isolation at home, relieved only by "brief stylized public appearances." Yet the island is also a place where men have "confined" women. Ostensibly, while the men are free to conduct their business and leisure as they desire, the women are "protected."[32]

The wooded paths of the island and the winding city streets provide a dialectical pattern that I have adapted in the screenplay as images that compel Edna beyond reason and intuition to revelation. In an uncustomary yet coherent reversal Edna wanders alone in both settings to escape her social constraints. In the city the anonymity of urban space offers inner solitude and brings repressed thoughts to the surface, while on the island Edna must retreat into nature to escape the restrictions of the social milieu.

One of the ways in which the contrasts of the city and the island are used to convey the theme of Edna's journey is through the extension of a single metaphor in both settings, the maze. I stress the labyrinth image because it provides a unifying visual metaphor of the "maze of inward contemplation" that Edna experiences on her circuitous journey to the center of the self. The maze image is most often represented by the weaving passage of the bayou and island terrain and by the intricate street patterns of New Orleans, which were designed to accommodate the twisting contours of the Mississippi.

The connection of the female and the labyrinth is often found in women's writings. One illustration is Anaïs Nin's insight that the city of Fez resembles women's mysterious, intuitive sensibility: "The layers of the City of Fez are like the layers of secrecies of the inner life." Nin uses the maze metaphor, "the labyrinth of the streets," to expose the secrets of women's hidden lives. In *A New Mythos: The Novel of the Artist as Heroine,* Grace Stewart relates how the recurring image of a journey to self-knowledge in women's fiction is represented by the labyrinth motif: "Most intriguing in the imagery of these journeys is the frequent mention of the labyrinth or maze, where the heroine faces dissolution or confronts her demon of destruction." Artistic integrity is maintained only through rebirth. In a study with a similar methodology Sharon Spencer explains how the attempt to search for a full life leads the artist/heroine to "travel the long, dark, tortuous path" that makes possible an "autonomous relationship to one's female self and to others." Kolodny also refers to the maze metaphor as a condition of the "fear of entrapment," noting that female protagonists tend to experience the world as an immense hieroglyph."[33]

As Edna winds her way through the labyrinthian paths and streets, the "psyche revealed through its relationship with the physical," important truths work their way to the surface. The female protagonists in several fine films by women directors are tracked on their long walks as a rendering of the inner self. Notable for this technique is Agnes Varda's *Cleo 5 to 7* in which seemingly trifling events are the core of the film: "The meaning of the film is taking place subterraneously. What we are seeing is the world as it might appear to someone whose very existence is in a state of suspension." Cleo's long walks signal the confusion and mystery that is often inevitable to women and mark her change from passivity to interest. Critics view Varda's technique here as a "breaking away from the over-organized cinema."[34]

Chopin gives Edna the experience of walking alone: "I [Edna] always feel so sorry for women who don't like to walk; they miss so much—so many rare little glimpses of life; and we women learn so little of life on the whole" (*CW,* 990). Edna's walks manifest her awareness that wandering occasioned: "She liked then to wander alone into strange and unfamiliar places" (*CW,* 940). The walking scenes in the screenplay convey a duality: Edna seems oblivious to her surroundings, yet at another level, she notices the secret lives of the passersby. Alone in her inner world, she tries to gain knowledge of herself as she mentally pursues these strangers. The shadowy and twisting streets lined with old narrow buildings reflect a sense of mystery and secret lives. Also, Edna's walks take on a far more dramatic meaning in view of the proscription against middle-class women's going about unescorted. Edna is an obvious anomaly in the commercial street crowd. Adding to the colorful array of street scenes were the rituals and drama of Congo Square, the center of black cultural life. Among the more interesting customs was the religious practice of voodoo, practitioners of which both races patronized. Some of the more famous voodoo rulers, such as Marie Laveau and her daughter, also known as Marie Laveau, invited prominent Creole men to their ceremonies. The queens lit candles, spoke curses and wrote them on slips of paper, and then danced around the altars while throngs attentively watched.[35] In the screenplay Edna's brief encounter at the voodoo parlor is a sign of the little-known alliance between the powerful black voodoo queens and the white matrons of New Orleans, who risked coming together in secret, despite the law against the assembling of white women and slaves. White men relied on the advice of these voodoo queens for their personal and professional decisions. For white women the alliance was a way of touching this intermediary of power over the patriarchs to form their own secret connections to voodoo. Chopin's era witnessed the descendance of voodoo in New Orleans, yet the city retained its influence as a mysterious element.

Edna's city walks serve two purposes. The street environment offers clues to her cultural dilemma, and the physical movement of the Quarter projects a sense of freedom. Thus the walking scenes bring forth an authentic flavor of the period, which in turn relates directly to Edna's situation.

The path to the beach, an island parallel of city streets in its labyrinthine contours, becomes the rural corridor in Edna's journey to self-knowledge. The description of the path lends itself to this interpretation: "[A] long, sandy path, upon which a sporadic and tangled growth that bordered it on either side made frequent and unexpected inroads" (CW, 894). The narrator says that it was "as if her [Edna's] thoughts had gone ahead of her and she was striving to overtake them" (CW, 995). Since the island path is a metaphor for Edna's state of mind, it is captured in the screenplay with low lingering ground shots that suddenly give way to partial views of Edna large in the frame. Her skirt trails; her hand brushes an overhead twig aside. The utter silence suggests how the anxiety and ambiguity of Edna's quest is perceived through the levels of quiet.

The marsh waterways are also metaphors of Edna's evolution. The most apt description of these mysterious and sheltered channels by Chopin is in her novel *At Fault*. A selection of Chopin's phrases from the novel suggests the gothic and decaying terrain: "A dull splash of some object falling," the "grim cypress and moss covered arms," and the "dim leafy tunnels" (*CW*, 750). This atmosphere is evoked in the screenplay when Edna and Robert return to Grand Isle from their sojourn on Chênière Caminada.

Arner suggests that Chopin uses the decay and age of the city's labyrinthine streets and the waterways of the Louisiana landscape to provide a link with ancient European chivalry, a cultural institution that also limited women's freedom. Through maze upon maze Chopin sought to convey Edna's despair and hope. Beneath the surface her struggle is urgent and complex, if unseen. Edna's movements are a significant aspect of the screenplay's action—trips taken on a small plane to enlarge her mind's realm. However, as interesting as they may be, the paths, inland waterways, and city streets are less powerful than Chopin's most significant metaphor, the sea.

In the screenplay the sea becomes a vivid mirror of Edna's consciousness. Critics have commented extensively on the mysterious effect of Chopin's sea, which the author treats through mythic, historical, and literary conventions as an eloquent metaphor of Edna's quest. In the sea Edna escapes the physical limitations of patriarchal culture. Her desire to learn to swim begins timidly and grows bolder as she becomes more determined to "part the tides of tradition," and Edna's elation when she masters the skill of swimming is a powerful transcendental moment.

It is difficult for us in our time, although we realize most sports excluded women, to understand just how dramatic is Edna's desire to learn to swim. In his social history of Louisiana sports Dale Somers relates how activists for women's rights used sports as a forum: "The American woman, trying to free herself from the confining aspects of Victorian society, saw participation in sports as a convenient method of vivifying her struggle for equality with men."

Women were discouraged from participation in sports through such varied means as exclusion from club memberships to insults. Swimming was a popular local activity because of the low cost and the warm climate. Women, however, encountered opposition when they used the beach and lake facilities. Somers quotes from a newspaper article that warns women of the "life-threatening" danger to them, such as toughening of the skin, quickening of the surface circulation of the blood, and accumulation of flesh and sinew.[36] Learning to swim is an authentic historical metaphor for Edna's search for independence.

In the water Edna reaches out for the unlimited in herself, and swims in a moment that Chopin thinks exceptional: "A feeling of exultation overtook her, as if some power of significant import had been given her to control the working of her body and her soul. She grew daring and reckless, overestimating her strength. She wanted to swim far out, where no woman had swum before" (CW, 908). This passage is the clearest and most powerful statement of Chopin's theme. Earlier, when Robert gives her lessons, Edna fears the sea as a symbol of the unknown knowledge that haunts her: "A certain ungovernable dread hung about her when in the water" (CW, 908). When Edna swims, Chopin compares her accomplishments to a child who in learning to walk "realize[s] its powers." The mastery of swimming is an ironic counterpoint to Chopin's earlier remark that "women are not granted much wisdom," because in the water Edna does gain both knowledge and control. This skill is the means to Edna's regeneration as an "artist/hero." Her struggle exemplifies the theme of woman's quest celebrated in stories from myth, history, and literature.

Annis Pratt points out that the idea of "communion with the authentic self" is achieved by the heroine in an epiphany with nature that "becomes a touchstone by which she holds herself together in the face of destructive roles proffered to her by society."[37] The choices offered Edna are so against her intuitive and reasoning powers that she seeks relief in the authenticity of nature. Although men might see learning to swim as a duel between themselves and nature, Edna sees it as a natural process.

If in the water Edna looks toward shore, on land she gazes at the sea. The seashore, the region between land and water, intrigued the

impressionists because of their intellectual preoccupation with inde-
finable space. In the screenplay I present the shore as a significant
demarcation between Edna and the unknown, between intuition
and reason, between Edna and others. The shore's constantly changing contours are a reminder of the pull between the self and the
demands of the culture. With typical ambiguity Chopin tempers
Edna's accomplishment. When the swimmer returns to shore, the
community awaits to restrain her and to deflect her newly gained
awareness. Léonce's behavior is particularly odd. Rather than con-
gratulating her, he subdues her joy with a laconic remark: "You were
not so far my dear, I was watching you" (CW, 909). This parentlike
deflation reminds Edna that Léonce is watching her to hold her
back. Mme Lebrun, as a representative of the others, calls Edna
capricious and remarks that she is not a "normal thinking and acting
creature." When Edna walks away seeking solitude to savor her accomplishment, the group attempts to restrain her: "They all called to
her and shouted to her." The ebb and flow of the sea at the shore
illustrate the dichotomy of the "shallow," which is the community,
and the "depth," which is Edna's experience.

The sea is a powerful reminder in Chopin of women's destiny. It is
described as a strong, unyielding force that in its constant ebb and
flow is both eternal and unpredictable. In the screenplay there is a
constant pull to the sea. It is in the basin of water rippled by Edna's
hands, and it is revealed in the watercolor on the cottage wall, as
well as in the spring rain's rivulet. Image appears within image, and
this technique alternately masks and reveals. Edna's quest, like the
sea, is irreconcilable: she lacks control of her destiny but controls her
quest; her relationship to the sea is essentially a psychological ven-
ture. She returns to the Lebrun cottage to ponder these realities.

Although the scenes of the screenplay move back and forth in
time, there is a constant forward thrust to illustrate Edna's development. On Grand Isle she takes on the challenge of swimming, and in
the city she dares to go walking alone. These parallel physical activities convey the vigor of her quest. The subtle experience of Edna
working on her art is more difficult to convey. It parallels her other
activities but is finally a more complex objective.

Many nineteenth-century paintings show women being tutored
in art or engaged in drawing, a typical Victorian accomplishment.

Art amused the family and provided a pleasant diversion for young women. But the serious woman artist, as Stewart finds, is isolated, vulnerable, and "imprisoned in the labyrinth by outside forces." These outside barriers represent the restrictions of culture that seek to punish women artists who attempt to live for their own self-interest: "Such actions on behalf of the artist self are, paradoxically, fatal to the self as woman."[38] Edna's strong sense of self, a characteristic celebrated in male artists, leads first to her unwillingness to compromise her own integrity, and ultimately to her paradoxically fatal act.

In women's literature the central character's search for authenticity is frequently linked to the development of meaningful and independent work. Because the writers are themselves "seeking artists" caught in the dilemma between the traditional role of a woman and the demands of the artistic life, their heroines also tend to have the artist's nature and ambition. Chopin often used the artist as a character in her work, and in The Awakening the woman as artist achieves her highest development. Edna's experience as an artist mirrors Chopin's own growth as a creator. Chopin "paint[ed] in words." The sole record of her struggle as a woman artist, besides several sparse recollections, is in Edna. It can even be said that Edna's destiny is a presentiment of Chopin's own, in that the critical denouncement of The Awakening deeply saddened and then silenced Chopin.

Edna announces, "I am becoming an artist. Think of it!" (CW, 946). To become more than a hobbyist requires daring, a view that Mlle Reisz announces. Later, Edna tells Mlle Reisz that the art dealer says her work "grows in force and individuality" (CW, 963). Chopin develops Edna from an earlier stage of being "devoid of ambition" to a concentration on "becoming an artist." The scene in which Edna paints Adèle and then angrily crumples the drawing is the most obvious example of how she uses her art to convey messages from her subconscious. Adèle is the embodiment of all that Edna is in rebellion against. She brings out from deep within Edna the growing awareness that she will be unable to create "a new self" that conforms to her conception of the essential self. Edna's portraits all represent some facet of her own preoccupation, the innocent integrity of the children, Alcée Arobin's freedom from responsibility, her father's relentless rigidity, and the even greater subordination of women of color.

Chopin also used Edna's painting to comment on her shifts of mood and of levels of awareness. Edna's artistic endeavor is solitary. Nowhere is this better shown than in the scene where she reluctantly asks Adèle for her untutored compliments. The metaphor of Edna as artist is a dramatic analogue to her inner mind and acts as a focus of the dialectical tensions. Edna absorbs her experience of the world and by taking her art as seriously as she dares to, recreates through her own artist's vision a more comprehensible reality. Edna is content when she paints; she thinks, changes, and learns. Even her dissatisfaction with results does not diminish her creative ebullience. Art is an important guide, but not a solution, to her quest toward authenticity. Ultimately art fails Edna.

Although Edna remains the central consciousness of the screenplay, the other characters still play crucial roles as "attitudes" of Edna. In particular, Adèle and Mlle Reisz are each central aspects of Edna's conflict. Adèle plays two important functions: she reminds Edna of the wifely and maternal role Edna seeks to subvert, and in a way that is natural to the Creole manner, she teaches Edna sensitivity to her physical self. Chopin's portrayal of Adèle appears to come straight from the social history of the era: "The Creole [woman] had gayety [sic], sentiment, spirit, with a certain climactic langour, sweetness of disposition, and charm of manner, and no seldom winning beauty; she was passionately fond of dancing and of music, and occasionally adept in the latter; and she had candor, and either simplicity or the art of it."[39] This description details the contrivances that formed the Creole woman. My characterization of Adèle treats her with more seriousness and allows a slight ambiguity to show in order to illustrate her importance to Edna's development. The focus is on the deep friendship between the two women and on Adèle's role as Edna's mentor in intimacy. Chopin's ironic touch is subdued, and consequently Adèle has more depth than her "mother-woman" image in the novel: "[women] idolized their children, worshiped their husbands, and esteemed it a holy privilege to efface themselves as individuals and grow wings as ministering angels" (CW, 888).

Adèle and Edna's friendship is a constant of the novel. Some critics note that the intensity of Edna's scenes with Robert pale when compared with her interactions with Adèle and conclude this means Edna is sexually immature. Kolodny shows, on the other hand, that Edna's choice is mature, based on the purpose of her quest rather than on traditional perceptions of male/female relationships. This idea is bolstered by Carroll Smith-Rosenberg's pioneering study of women's relationships with each other in nineteenth-century America.[40] Deeply felt closeness and intimacy expressed in sensual affection with an absence of sexual connotations symbolized the distinct separateness of "woman's place/man's world." The narrator in *The Awakening* remarks of the relationship between the two women: "Who can tell what metals the gods use in forging the subtle bond which we call sympathy, which we might as well call love" (*CW*, 894). To convey their relationship I invert one of Chopin's picturesque metaphors from a short story in which a shy lover tenderly caresses his beloved with a rose. When Edna visits her friend, Adèle shows her affection by passing a rose over Edna's face. Most often in Victorian era fiction women view other women as competitors for men or as mirrors through which men reflect their own ideas and behavior. Edna and Adèle's friendship represents a different model; with each other they are caring, serious, and loyal.

In the beach scene Adèle leads Edna from apathy to feeling: "[S]he soon lent herself readily to the Creole's gentle caress" (*CW*, 897). Edna leans her head on Adèle's shoulder: "She was flushed and felt intoxicated with the sound of her own voice and the unaccustomed taste of candor. It muddled her like wine, or like a first breath of freedom" (*CW*, 899). Edna regards Adèle as a "sensuous madonna." On Chênière Caminada, Edna explores her friend's advice to become more physically aware and studies her own reflection "as if it were something she saw for the first time" (*CW*, 918). This moment initiates an awakening. The physical rapport between the two women is the mirror opposite of a scene with Robert in which Edna rejects his attempt to rest his head against her arm: "She did not remonstrate, except again to repulse him quietly but firmly" (*CW*, 891). Only once, when they kiss in their final meeting, do Edna and Robert come physically close to each other. On at least three occasions, Chopin shows that Robert is an intruder in the intimate friendship between Edna and Adèle. His arrival in the beach scene ends the women's private talk; Edna twice repulses his touch when the three are together; and finally, Edna chooses Adèle over Robert in the novel's penultimate episode. Edna fantasizes about Robert when she is with him and when they are apart. The one day they spend together on Chênière Caminada, Edna drowses in church, sleeps away the afternoon, and then dreamily sails home. After Robert departs to Mexico, he becomes stronger in her daydreams and is an absent focus of her other relationships. The narrator remarks, "As Edna walked along the street she was thinking of Robert" (*CW*, 936). She also speaks of him to Mlle Reisz and to Mme Lebrun. Chopin's narrative subtly supports this interpretation, as Cynthia Griffin Wolff noticed.[41] For example, Edna summons "into her spiritual vision the presence of the beloved one" (*CW*, 972). She wants Robert's spirit, his configuration. When Robert returns from Mexico Edna seems eager to see him, yet when they do meet, she muses: "But some way he had seemed nearer to her off there in Mexico" (*CW*, 987).

There is a quite similar aspect to Edna's relationships with Alcée Arobin.[42] During the scene of their intimacy he complains after she discusses Mlle Reisz, "I desired to talk of you," and Edna responds in irritation that he can if he must, "but let me *think* [emphasis added] of something else while you do" (*CW*, 966).

Adèle, on the other hand, is a nurturing influence and, therefore, a more powerful character. The preeminence of Adèle in Edna's life has its most fateful moment when Edna decides between her "long awaited *dream* [emphasis added]" of being with Robert or going to Adèle as she awaits childbirth. Despite Robert's pleading for her to stay, she chooses Adèle. "I must go to my friend," she tells him. This decision reflects Adèle's role as guide to Edna's discovery of her natural feelings. Then later, when Edna leaves Adèle, she feels despondent because she has arrived at an inescapable conclusion about women's destiny. She expects that Robert will be waiting for her inside the house, but as she converses outside with the doctor there is no anticipation in her attitude. Robert is simply no longer in her thoughts. Edna is depressed even before she realizes Robert has left.

The development of Edna's sensual self parallels her journey toward self-knowledge. That it was natural for Adèle to play a crucial role is a cultural aspect of Victorian women's relationships, as Smith-Rosenberg points out. In her nurturing role, Adèle is limited only in that she automatically parrots the restrictions of their culture. She admonishes Edna to abandon her activity outside the home, cautions her against rumor, and urges her to think of the children.

Mlle Reisz is Chopin's most stereotypical character. She is eccentric and without social or physical graces. Because it is assumed no man would want this type of woman, she is free to pursue her art. I subdue her homeliness so that attention focuses on her relation to Edna as a committed artist. It is misleading to assume that she is a "failed woman" in her unmarried state. Perhaps Mlle Riesz chose her life, even with its flaws, over the constraints of marriage. After all, it is Mlle Reisz who tells Edna, "I should never deem a man of ordinary caliber worthy of my devotion" (*CW*, 964).

Mme Ratignolle and Mlle Reisz function as a contrasting pair. Adèle with her excessive femininity, exaggerated beauty and selfless family devotion contrasts sharply with the pianist's lack of feminine conformity, devotion to her art, and solitary lifestyle. These two friends suggest the polar extremes between which Edna must choose. The domestic harmony of the Ratignolle home causes Edna to feel "appalling and hopeless ennui." She thinks her friend has never "tasted of life's delirium." Mlle Reisz has the "courageous soul" of the true artist, but lives without love or society. She also qualifies her regard for Edna's artistic aspirations by tempering her advice with warnings rather than offering encouragement. It is interesting to speculate on why Chopin, who enjoyed both her artistic life and an active social circle, drew Mlle Riesz in such stark terms as a "disagreeable little woman" who quarrels with everyone and has a bad disposition and the ambiguous "temper which was self-assertive" (*CW*, 905). She is the one, however, whom Edna seeks out as a mentor, and Edna later deflects Alcée's criticism of her by saying, "She seems to me wonderfully sane" (*CW*, 966). Everything in Chopin's oeuvre must be checked against irony. I believe Mlle Reisz is portrayed out of anger as a comic stereotype of the unmarried woman with a profession, as, for example, Henry James's individualistic female characters are portrayed out of hostility.

The culture's rigid stratifications leave Edna without an alternative. In her own life Chopin experienced both choices, but not, of course, at the same time. While married she gave birth to six children in nine years, in that sense even more like a "mother-woman" than Adèle. The narrator tells us Adèle has been married for seven years, has three children, and is pregnant again—"about every two years she had a baby" (CW, 889). When widowed, Chopin developed her writing career.

Chopin's other characters also appear in the screenplay as analogues of Edna's mental quest and as proof of the cultural limitations that restrict her development. Léonce, the main representation of Edna's oppression, is sketched in few words. He wears "eye glasses" and "he stoop[s] a little." In short, he is not particularly attractive, at least not to Edna, but in one of the novel's subtle inversions it is her indifference that draws Edna to Léonce. It allows her to use her energy to think: "[She] realize[s] with some unaccountable satisfaction that no trace of passion or excessive and fictitious warmth colored her affection, thereby threatening its dissolution" (CW, 898). The inverted dialectic serves to safeguard their relationship, giving Edna the freedom to ponder her situation.

Critics have commented that Edna's rebellion is unwarranted because Léonce's behavior is not overtly cruel; however, Chopin's quarrel with tradition is based on control by the force of social custom. As long as women's subjugation is upheld, the facade of mutual contentment is maintained. On Grand Isle Léonce is mostly absent, and in New Orleans he is present only in the scenes that illustrate the disparity between male and female roles. Once Chopin has portrayed Léonce's patriarchal expectations and Edna's resistance, his physical presence is no longer required.

If Léonce is arrogant, it is because society has cast him this way. In Chopin's era it was revolutionary enough to suggest the restructuring of women's roles without perceiving the male as the victim of narrow options as well. Typical character traits found in descriptions of nineteenth-century Creole men include "pride, intolerance of criticism, love of family and the old order of things, unprogressiveness, vehemence, and easily-aroused ire. But if these men were somewhat intolerant, they still possessed nobility of character, big-heartedness and urbanity."[43] Léonce is the Creole ideal, dedicated to business and devoted to family. To give Edna's conflict more immediacy I endow Léonce with greater depth.

One of the ways Chopin plays with opposition is in her portrayal of Alcée Arobin, who signifies a mild mockery of Creole male standards, having neither business nor family and respecting neither. These contrasts are part of a pattern that helps Edna to realize that tradition is variable, and therefore social customs may be questioned.

Creole men also had the "capacity to master, a trait developed during the era of slavery."[44] One of the ways in which Chopin conveys this tendency to control is through her use of the ritual of smoking as a male prerogative. Smoking fascinated Chopin. She used it both to dramatize men's authority and to illustrate women's flaunting of the male code. In her own life she delighted in this unconventional habit and gave it enough importance to remark about it several times in her journals and essays. In one article she satirically claims to have "disguised myself as a gentleman smoking cigars with my feet on the table" (CW, 700). In Chopin's short story "An Egyptian Cigarette," a woman with an androgynous personality smokes alone in her train compartment and dreams of exotic and disturbing scenes abetted by the smoke that fills the room (CW, 571). In many ways, this story written the year before The Awakening prefigures the novel's themes.

Whenever Edna and Léonce are together he smokes. As the two quarrel over the restrictions of Creole life smoke creates a "mist" that connotes Léonce's ignorance of Edna's needs. One scene has a particularly amusing irony. Edna disobeys Léonce and stays outside in the hammock; then he joins her on the porch, where he remains after Edna finally goes inside. Léonce retains his dignity having usurped her solitude. He smokes leisurely and a "misty puff of smoke fills the night air" (CW, 913).

Smoking also provides a counterpoint to Edna's growing awareness of male behavior. On several occasions Léonce gives Robert a cigar, which the latter always pockets rather than join Léonce in a smoke. When Robert returns from Mexico he smokes a cigar and has a smoking pouch. This development parallels Edna's realization that the two men have more in common than she at first realized. Robert conveys his traditional masculine attitude when he recoils as Edna exclaims that she "is no longer one of Mr. Pontellier's possessions" (CW, 992).

In the screenplay I use the "misty puffs of smoke" to emphasize that men are the agents of women's social limitations. I also use smoking to suggest the daring of women who smoked to usurp male territory. I give Edna a cigarette to hold, for example, during a moment of revelation at the Grand Isle dinner party, the unlit cigarette a reflection of her yearning for independence.

One of the more complex characterizations of a minor character is Chopin's Dr. Mandelet, modeled after her own friend, Dr. Frederick Kolbenheyer. Critics have had a difficult time with Dr. Mandelet. I present him as neither the disguised chauvinist nor the ignored savior, two poles in Chopin criticism, but as an empathetic yet limited friend who goes further in understanding Edna than do the other characters. Léonce dominates her. Adèle warns her to conform. Mlle Reisz patronizes her ambition. Yet even with his compassion and genuine fondness for Edna, he is incapable of understanding the complexity of her struggle. When she rejects the chance to confide in Dr. Mandelet, it is because she has become awakened to her predicament. The screenplay opens with a scene in which Dr. Mandelet receives a notice announcing Edna's death. This seemed to me a succinct way to state the theme. Nothing in Edna's culture will assist her in reaching her objective, not even Dr. Mandelet's empathetic tendencies.

In this scene I use a ritual of the Vieux Carré to add depth both to the sense of futility of Edna's quest and to Dr. Mandelet's role as the most understanding supporting character. When someone died every post carried the news on black-bordered posters, and formal invitations to the funeral were hand delivered in silver baskets by servants in ornate uniforms. In Chopin's short story "The Godmother," a death notice is "bordered in black and decorated with an old-fashioned woodcut of a weeping willow beside a grave" (CW, 614). The heavy frame provides a clue that people cannot break out of cultural obstructions easily. It is dialectical because the tree and the border contrast with the theme of social constraint opposed to natural ways.

Each of Chopin's supporting characters, no matter how minimally sketched, seems integral to Edna's development. In the novel the link between identity and motherhood is all-encompassing, yet when Edna's sons do appear it is through her perspective, and children are actually given a very minor place. Raoul and Etienne have a larger role in the screenplay in order to emphasize Edna's classic dilemma— her alternation between love for the children and her wish to be free of the constant care of them. With the decision to give the Pontelliers sons rather than daughters Chopin adds weight to the motherhood dilemma. Victorian culture classified children as small adults. As "little men," Raoul and Etienne may represent another barrier to Edna's self-assertion. As is Léonce, the children in the screenplay are innocent victims of the restricted roles Victorian parents were destined to uphold.

Edna's two sisters, who are only referred to and who never appear in the novel, represent Edna's conflict of conformity and rebellion in its childhood origins. The narrator says, "Margaret—she has all the Presbyterianism undiluted. And the youngest is something of a vixen" (CW, 948). I place them in the screenplay as children in church and in Edna's reverie in the beach scene to provide a context for Edna's dwelling on the past as a way to think about the future.

Women of color, in the many variations of Louisiana race culture, silent or absent, provide the domestic work force that makes possible the Creole lifestyle. They are nursemaids, cooks, launderers, servants in every capacity. Anna Shannon Elfenbein suggests that Chopin understands more about the dark women of the novel than Edna does, because she endows them "with an inner consciousness at variance with their forced conformity to the roles they play." Thus, the "fictitious animation" of the nursemaid to the Pontellier children. The presence of the servant women "illuminates the precariousness of Edna's status as an object of male desire, possession, and protection."[45] The silent servitude of these women dramatically points up what Edna stands to lose, as an upper-class woman, in renouncing her husband's class privilege and economic status. In a materialistic culture it is rather extraordinary to find that when Edna chooses to leave behind the symbols of Léonce's affluence and to move into the cottage, Chopin asserts she has gained: "There was a feeling of having descended in the social scale, with a corresponding sense of having risen in the spiritual" (CW, 977). By having a bourgeois woman as an emblem of self-assertion, Chopin shows how women's status is dependent on male standing and goodwill and is therefore an insecure and illusionary position. As Edna tells Mlle Reisz: "The house, the money that provides for it, are not mine" (CW, 962).

Another way in which Chopin "sees more than Edna" about racism is that the male characters tell "tales" about lower-class women that imply the women count for little beyond sexual purposes. This risqué bragging confuses Edna. Although, as noted, minority women are largely silent or absent, they are a powerful indictment in the novel of the range of oppression.

Characterization is a strength of Kate Chopin's. I never considered eliminating any one of these interesting minor players or felt compelled to introduce new characters as adapters often do. Together, Chopin's supporting characters comprise a unified background for Edna's foreground role.

Another strength of Chopin's is her use of symbols, which for their era, have a startling visual context. Arner anticipates this when he notes that the novel's symbols exist "to express, as nearly as possible the inexpressible, to indicate areas of meaning lying beyond the province of language proper." Tompkins also refers to Chopin's "dense configuration of images that echo, reinforce, contradict and enrich one another with tantalizing suggestiveness and an unparalleled economy of means." *The Awakening* then, somewhat extraordinarily, as compact as it is, contains a world of material objects and allusions that both illustrate the era and reveal Edna's situation. The most commented on metaphor is women's apparel, a cohesive symbol of the restrictive social code. The historian Helene Roberts points out that the "clothing of the Victorian woman clearly projected the message of a willingness to conform to the submissive-masochistic pattern, but dress also helped mold female behavior to the role of the 'exquisite slave' [Thackeray]." Clothing accentuated traits of inactivity, frivolity, submissiveness, and delicateness. Very wide or hobbled skirts, fragile fabrics, high heels, elaborate hair dress, pocket books, and parasols all announced that the wearer could not possibly put forth physical effort. Apparel styles were not only awkward, they could be dangerous. Among the more debilitating practices was the "corset culture," as it came to be known. The tightly laced garments caused many physical problems, from an inability to move around to serious disorders such as spinal defects, lung disease, and maternal ailments, including infant mortality. The crinoline was another fashionable garment, which according to Roberts "transformed women into caged birds surrounded by hoops of steel." Several Chopin critics have remarked on the caged-bird imagery of *The Awakening*, which Peter Petersen believes represents "controlled and perverted nature" and implies the estrangement of women from their natural inclinations; they are also "caged."[46]

Chopin describes women's dress in detail, using patterns of dress and undress to illustrate the connection between clothes and status, a narrative device easily translated to film images. Edna was becoming herself, Chopin writes, "and daily casting aside that fictitious self which we assume like a garment with which to appear before the world" (*CW*, 939). Several examples will demonstrate Chopin's method. Edna often alters or changes her attire at epiphanic moments. On the beach with Adèle at the onset of an introspective reverie, she "removed her collar and opened her dress at the throat" (*CW*, 895). In her desire for relief she contrasts sharply with the impeccable and fussy Adèle, who remains swathed in veil and gauntlets. As Edna prepares to nap on Chênière Caminada she "loosened her clothes, removing the greater part of them" (*CW*, 917). She later awakens with a changed consciousness.

In the scene in which Robert prepares to depart for Mexico, Edna is disturbed, and characteristically she "change[s] her gown for a more comfortable and commodious wrapper" (*CW*, 924). She then pointedly stays alone to sort out her thoughts. The people around Edna notice the implications of these costume changes. Adèle senses the rejection her comfortable state implies. Léonce first notices that something is amiss in the reception day scene when he finds Edna "not in her usual reception gown, [but rather] in an ordinary house dress" (*CW*, 932). The changes of dress from formal to informal emphasize Edna's inner stress and development and in one sense prefigure her freest moment: "All the tearing emotions of the last few hours seemed to fall away from her like a somber, uncomfortable garment, which she had but to loosen to be rid of" (*CW*, 996).

Arner comes close to making a filmic observation when he remarks on Chopin's style of "zooming in" on some concrete object that represents the action.[47] A particularly fine example occurs in the first chapter. The reader is introduced to Edna through her "white sunshade that was advancing at a snail's pace" (*CW*, 882). The objectification of Edna through her paraphernalia indicates that she is indeed defined by external reality. In other words, the emotional content of objects and characters is similar: Edna's sunshade is as much a metaphor of Victorian womanhood as is Adèle Ratignolle.

Such diverse items as Mlle Riesz's wilted violets and Adèle's lace handkerchiefs contribute to distinct characterization and also provide visual significance.

Among other material contexts that illustrate Edna's states of mind and that the screenplay draws upon is the scene where the Pontelliers quarrel over Edna's neglect of her reception day, after which she retreats to the bedroom. There, in intense agitation, she contemplates her feelings and thoughts. She gazes out the window at the dark "deep jungle of the garden below." The garden, "a dark and alluring labyrinth," is a metaphor for the human mind.[48] She is "seeking herself and finding herself" (CW, 934). Edna's complex thoughts spin out through the "tortuous outline of flowers and foliage" into the night. Gardens and flowers, so important in Creole culture, illustrate a range of moods and ideas in the adaptation.

Other elements in this episode convey absorbing Victorian ideas but are too melodramatic for the screenplay when combined with the vividness of the night garden imagery. Their effect would be too obvious and would mar the seriousness of Edna's reflections. For example, when Edna flings her wedding band away she is obviously rebelling against female confinement. The vase is another Victorian literary metaphor and commonly symbolizes female chastity. In a "sweeping passion" Edna flings the vase to the hearth. The broken vase signals the end of Edna and Léonce's relationship. However, Edna's deliberate expression of temper in this scene is incongruous. These melodramatic "stage properties," the wedding band, the vase, and the lace handkerchief, are omitted in the screenplay in favor of a more unified and complex approach. The garden is brought into the room with one symbolic flower and linked to the ring as a motif of Edna's dilemma through an unconscious gesture: Edna removes her ring and repeatedly slips it back and forth over the flower stem.

Certain other episodes and props of the novel are embellished in the screenplay to articulate Edna's inner self in filmic terms. The novel's hammock and a stereoscope, an object that I add to the screenplay, illustrate this point. Chopin's hammock has historic relevance. Women posed in hammocks were a popular theme for illustrations between the 1830s and the 1860s. A typical drawing featured a partially nude woman lying on her back in a languorous pose with her bodice undone. These illustrations catered to erotic fantasy and were reproduced by the hundreds. As art historians have noted, the images represented the removal of the woman from the boudoir to the outdoors, the hammock serving as a substitute for the bed.[49] In *The Awakening* Chopin reverses the traditional meaning. When Edna lies in the hammock Chopin writes that "she was not a supercilious or an over-dainty woman. She was not much given to reclining in the hammock, and when she did so it was with no catlike suggestion of voluptuous ease, but with a beneficent repose which seemed to invade her whole body" (*CW*, 910).

In several important scenes of revelation—for example, after her exultant swim—Edna seeks the hammock. Its sway echoes the water's movement and connects swimming to rocking in a continuity of development. When Léonce entreats her to come inside, the hammock becomes the site of Edna's successful defiance: "With a writhing motion she settled herself more securely in the hammock" (*CW*, 912). This narrative suggests a subtle yet radical transformation. In a visual sense the "writhing motion" marks Edna's passage from her accustomed passivity to a rebellious yet restrained independence. In negating the familiar image, Chopin provides a visual metaphor for Edna's assertion of self. The learning process occurs and recurs in actions of seeking through nature, with objects that symbolize both women's oppression and Edna's rebellion.

A less dramatic but equally relevant and visually appealing metaphor of the times is the stereoscope. During the 1880s the stereoscope gained popularity with the upper class who enjoyed it as a leisure time pursuit. Most popular were photographs of distant locales and of scenic areas. The absence in Edna's life of concrete tasks leaves her long periods of time when she does not paint, swim, walk, or attend the races. The stereoscope expresses Edna's interest in the world beyond her narrow realm and, in a sense, symbolizes her quest. It is a way to focus on the indolence of women's routines and to extend Edna's artistic sensibilities.

In the screenplay, the stereoscope also becomes a visual analogue for the important fiction reading in the novel. For example, Edna reads French novelists, such as Daudet, on Grand Isle, but as she becomes more herself the Creole influence lessens. Later she reads Emerson. In the screenplay, Edna views foreign scenes, and as time passes she looks at popular views of the American West, a sequence that is intended to illustrate developing individuality.

In the novel, as Edna's conflict heightens, the field of events opens. The tumultuous arena of horse racing and the jeopardy of an affair symbolize Edna's inner state. In the screenplay these expressions of feelings are shown by parallel shots of movement, for example, trains speeding by and horses galloping. One of the more interesting actions within the novel to transpose to a visual analogue is Chopin's use of horse racing. The screenplay brings the scenes of Edna and horse racing from an aside to a central event. This transposition accomplishes several visual motifs. Aspects of the site itself, patron seating arrangements, and the horse race all signify diverse conditions of the restrictive social code. The racetrack played an important role in Creole society. The five thousand acres beyond Lake Pontchartrain, which came to be known as the Fair Grounds, were originally the estate of the de Marigny family. This vivid forest had "tall pines, interspersed with spruce, sweet gum, and the dramatic bloom of magnolia. At intervals rose gnarled oaks, and about them twisted slow bayous."[50]

During the Civil War the grounds fell into disuse, but later when the city recovered, wealthy Creoles formed a partnership to build the famous Jockey Club on the site and to revitalize the park. There were beautiful fountains, gardens, a promenade for the fashionable guests, and a three-tiered grandstand that seated five thousand. The grandstand was divided into three separate sections, one for male members, one for the men of the general public, and one for ladies, who were admitted by special invitation only. The racetrack segregation provides a dramatic visual connection between the race and the spectators as a metaphor of Edna's conflict.

In life Edna will gamble a known security against unknown possibilities to circumvent cultural restrictions. In other words, the Edna who has cultivated the skills of the horse race spectator will also learn to take risks in life. In what is regarded as a man's world, Edna shows that she excels. Chopin suggests that only a lack of opportunity keeps women from achieving their potential. Edna is her most accomplished and vigorous self at the track. Her skill also provides an opportunity for her to have money of her own. In the screenplay, her success draws the attention of the other characters, and at the same time, it emphasizes the double standard of Creole society. Her track experience reminds the viewer that no matter how Edna struggles she will be held back by tradition. The race itself is centered on a beautiful and physically powerful animal that is also prized, tamed, and cultivated to perform under men's rule. As the horse speeds forward and around the track in a circle and then is returned to its stall, so Edna, and women in general, lead frustrating lives. History and metaphor merge to dramatize Edna's predicament.

I add trains to the screenplay because they in fact connected New Orleans to lower Louisiana where travelers could board a steamer to the islands. In Chopin's novel *At Fault*, trains are important symbols of the intrusion of civilization on the preferred natural world. A character listens to the "constant trains of cars speeding somewhere" and thinks that if he were at the wheel he would drive until the end was "death and chaos!" (*CW*, 785). Another example is in the story "Charlie" when the protagonist thinks that the "rhythm of the iron wheels seemed to mock her" (*CW*, 663). Chopin believed that the way technology is used debases the natural order. In her work it becomes a negative symbol of masculine culture. I use trains as an analogue of Edna's inner state as she speeds through the familiar landscape toward a resolution of her quest. The train combines many of Chopin's themes—the power of male culture, the conflict between nature and humankind, and the unremitting journey into destiny. I pair Edna with a train to objectify both her powerlessness and the determination of her final journey. Trains are also used in the screenplay as a connecting link between scenes in the city and scenes on Grand Isle.

I have yet to discuss adaptation issues presented by film's reliance on sound—dialogue, situational sound, and music. As Robbe-Grillet notes, "What has most escaped the powers of literature: which is not so much the image as the sound track—the sound of voices, noises, atmospheres, music—and above all the possibility of acting on two senses at once, the eye and the ear." Because authentic cinematic dialogue is difficult to write, adapters have relied on various conversion methods, of which the test of fidelity is a central issue. Richard Roud describes one style evident in Pinter's adaptation of *The Go-Between:* "Pinter did not write much new dialogue. But what he has done, often only by cutting a word or a line here and there, is to create his own very special brand of what the Greeks called Stechomythia . . . achieving of rhythm and speed through alternation." The original is compressed, and tone is retained, while a new form is composed with dialogue meant to be spoken instead of merely read. Joseph Gomez finds Kenneth Russell to be another adapter striving for an "accur[acy] to the spirit of the words," while "form[ing] a new structure appropriate to the film medium."[51]

The Awakening is a fascinating model with which to attempt the transposition from literary to cinematic dialogue, as well as for other aural cues. Chopin is recognized for her ability to reproduce "actual speech" and to replicate the many classes and idioms she heard as a transplanted Louisianan. Her French heritage, habit of intense observation, and interest in language all contributed to the acuity of her writing style. In *The Awakening* there is a gradual shift from French cultural references to more American ideas. For example, Eliane Jasenas compares the use of French idioms and English phraseology based on French grammar in the Grand Isle chapters with the fading away of French in the New Orleans chapters.[52] On Grand Isle, Chopin writes, Edna "had long wished to try herself on Mme Ratignolle" (*CW,* 891), and in New Orleans she thinks, "I'm not going to be forced into doing things" (*CW,* 995). This linguistic duality dramatizes Edna's internal conflict. Not only is Creole society restrictive, but it is not Edna's natural domain. Thus, her casting off of French culture is analogous to her search for her authentic self. In the screenplay I embellish this pattern as a subtle overlay of meaning in juxtaposition to the scenes moving back and forth in time. The effect matches that part of Edna's development that becomes awakened more through her intuitive sense than through reasoning. Speech patterns are beneath the surface of conscious awareness.

The novel's dialogue is sparing and used tellingly. Much of the action takes place in Edna's consciousness, and exchanges between characters are minimal. Chopin's language is interesting on a variety of levels. For example, she uses the genderless phrase "its powers" in a description of a child rather than the standard "his." When the Lebrun guests tell Edna that Léonce is the best of husbands she appears to agree, yet what Edna actually says is, "She was *forced* [emphasis added] to admit that she knew of none better" (*CW,* 887).

The dialogue highlights Edna's conflict. When Robert invites her for a swim she says, "Oh, no," but later joins him, obeying "one of the two contradictory impulses which impelled her" (*CW*, 893).

Chopin's text is rich in other linguistic devices; for example, she uses repetition and alliteration skillfully. When Léonce and Edna quarrel at dinner the word "out" appears repeatedly. It functions as a pun on the couple's state of mind in an otherwise superficial talk.[53] Phrases from the exchange include, "Tired out, Edna," "I was out," "Out! What could have taken you out?" "I simply felt like going out, and I went out" and "I told Joe to say I was out" (*CW*, 932). The rhythm builds and reinforces the point that these two are at "outs" with each other and linguistically illustrates how, although they speak the same language, they are beyond understanding. Such devices have a contemporary tone; for example, Beckett's *Waiting For Godot* has comparable dialogue.

Chopin also uses direct dialogue to counterpoint the action. The most ambiguous example occurs in the last chapter. Edna appears to be very interested in the dinner menu just moments before she will swim out to her death, "I'm very hungry," she says to Victor (*CW*, 908). Such intrusions on the logic of the moment add to the psychological depth of Edna's dilemma. Edna's chance remark seems to imply that she is "hungry," but not with a hunger that will be appeased by food. The remark also shows how Edna must consider the code against intruding one's problems on others and the preferred convention of pretense. There is literally no one she can trust. Her total isolation is poignant, as other critics have also noticed. It is the prelude to a tragic and authentic moment, and the final irony is moving. "Don't get anything extra," Edna politely advises Victor. Chopin uses this rather morbid exchange to comment on how Edna leaves behind the chivalric conventions that have entrapped her as she turns her back on Victor and Mariequita.

One of the more interesting problems of dialogue involves the temptation to draw on certain of Edna's speeches and thoughts that express dissatisfaction with women's role. Perhaps the most widely quoted of these is Edna's attempt to explain to Adèle the validity of a woman maintaining a degree of independence from her children: "I would give up the unessential; I would give my money, I would give my life for my children; but I wouldn't give myself" (*CW*, 929). Another example is Edna's assertion of her marital independence, "I am no longer one of Mr. Pontellier's possessions to dispose of or not. I give myself where I choose" (*CW*, 992). I omit such polemical dialogue from the screenplay because to include it is to invite artifice. Such narration is not conversational. This is apparent in many otherwise fine films based on literature, of which *The Bell Jar* is but one example. Sylvia Plath wrote narrative, such as the well-known "arrow shooting off" speech, which when read is both perceptive and humorous; however, its faithful transition to the screen renders it flat.

I use expressive and pertinent words and phrases from Chopin's fiction, essays, unpublished poetry and journals to present a mingled flow of "spoken" dialogue that preserves the tone of the original and expresses my emphasis on Edna's quest. The dialogue is a true amalgamation from various sources; some of the language is Chopin's own and some my own writing, which is both original and adapted from social history documents.

An example of the use of Chopin's other works is Edna's dreamlike abstraction, "Yet do the shades come without the sun," a line from Chopin's verse. Edna realizes that her mood, between despair and enlightenment, reflects the inaccessibility of her yearning for authenticity. Thinking out loud she cannot say exactly what it is she seeks, yet intuitively she knows it is as authentic as nature.

In those scenes with invented dialogue, I often rely on historical references. One such illustration is based on the corruption that flourished during Chopin's era and that everyone discussed with relish. Cash and lottery tickets exchanged hands on the streets, while political debates raged between factions in city hall. In 1891 Mayor Joseph A. Shakspeare conducted a reform against the powerful and corrupt Louisiana Lottery Company. The entire populace joined in, and the struggle took months to resolve. The mayor eventually won, many say, on his appeal to the Creole aristocrats regarding the "commonness" of the lottery. It is natural for M. Ratignolle to tell his wife over lunch the news he has heard that morning in the pharmacy.

In creating dialogue I kept in mind the more interesting linguistic analyses of women's writing, and in particular of Chopin's language. Although many critics in the last decade have embellished the ideas of the first wave of feminist literary criticism, I find Kolodny's discovery of reflexive perception in women's writing fresh and stimulating. Defined as a lack of self-awareness disclosed by grammatical form, reflexive perception occurs when a woman character finds herself in a situation she had not planned or cannot fully comprehend. Her amputated self-perception "explores and reveals a character's internal and subconscious dilemmas." It is a characteristic of the narrative that grammatically objectifies the character through a linguistic notation, rather like an excision of self from self. To illustrate this device Kolodny quotes from Margaret Atwood, "I must be crying then" and "I was surprised to find my feet moving." This linguistic disjunction is also found in *The Awakening,* such as in one of Edna's crying scenes, where "she could not have told us why she was crying" (*CW,* 886). Studies in women and men's oral speech find a lack of assertive self-expression in women aligned with feelings of social marginality.[54]

Language in *The Awakening* is a focus of the novel's most original recent criticism. Particularly instructive is Jean Wyatt's exploration of the psychodynamics of reading. Wyatt finds in the novel a revolutionary and semiotic language that "thwart[s] the capacity to decipher sentences according to known linguistic codes and throw[s] the reader into a state similar to Edna's."[55] She refers to Chopin's language of abstraction, which withdraws meaning because Edna's feelings cannot be clarified, "like a shadow, like a mist passing across her soul's summer day." For the novel's most elusive linguistic abstractions, the screenplay employs an imagery of seemingly illogical images. For example, the sea remains perfectly still while Edna's hair is whipped about her face. Is there a breeze or not? As Edna walks to the café in the city, sea birds appear overhead and startle her. Does she see them or recall them? A tropical flower—emblematic of southern womanhood—that has decorated the dinner table suddenly turns into a shell. Then the shell disappears, and Edna gazes into empty space. These images are part of a pattern that links Edna's imagination to her conflict between patriarchal structure and the insecurity of belief in a realm outside traditional territory.

Just as elusive are the "sounds" of the novel, the most persistent and haunting of which is the sea's murmuring refrain. Joan Clatworthy observes that the sea "is essentially untranslatable except as a non-verbal aural image in the reader's imagination."[56] The voice of the sea has its own emotive force and is an echoing refrain in the first half of the novel. Sea sounds follow Edna to the city as a reminder of the quest that she began to understand on the island. The world of experience and the world of intuition reflect each other in the murmuring voices of Edna's imagination. They have a musical tone and are contrapuntal in arrangement. When Edna retreats to her bedroom she hears discordant voices: "They jeered and sounded mournful notes without promise, devoid even of hope" (*CW*, 934). The scene of the dinner party is underscored by the fountain softly splashing in the garden: "Outside the soft, monotonous splash of a fountain could be heard; the sound penetrated into the room" (*CW*, 972). These "voices" in the background underscore Edna's alienation from the scene around her. The mood of forced gaiety suddenly changes to a "hopeless feeling."

Other situational sounds abound, drawn from Chopin's life—the sounds of nature, place, and people. There are the birds' calls, the piano's notes, the band at Klein's heard from a distance in the moonlight air. There is the talk, the laughter, the children at play, and the songs. Street vendors call their wares. Again, I rely on historical sources and draw on descriptions of pineapple vendors, lavender boys, and other characters and customs of the social milieu to provide an aura like the one Chopin knew. Sound was a constant refrain. Chopin's most direct autobiographical reference is found in "Mrs. Mobrey's Reason":

[C]ertain sounds, scenes, impressions move me I know, because I feel it. . . . There's nothing that has the meaning for me in this world that sound has. I feel as if the Truth were going to come to me, some day, through the harmony of it. I wonder if anyone else has an ear so tuned and sharpened as I have, to detect the music, not of the spheres, but of earth, subtleties of major and minor chord that the wind strikes upon the tree branches. (*CW*, 72–73)

Chopin was well schooled in music and it played an immutable role in her life, as Arner relates in "Music from A Farther Room." He traces Chopin's musical background and uses the theme of music to interpret her work, locating in *The Awakening* a symphonic structure: "The voice of the sea is heard and the enchantment of the night is felt at unpredictable but emotionally related intervals that soon establish a rhythm of their own, counterpointing the narrative pattern." Music as the "emblem of the self that lurks within" is part of Edna's longing to return to a world free of unnatural traditions.[57] Chopin suggests that music connects human beings to their natural selves.

In the novel music arises from events. When Mlle Reisz plays the piano to entertain, Edna experiences a "keen tremor." It is an epiphanic moment, "perhaps the first time her being was tempered to take an impress of abiding truth" (*CW*, 906). The music here is a refrain of her emotions. Later in the novel, when Edna's inner turmoil has intensified, she listens again to Mlle Reisz's playing: "The music grew strange and fantastic—turbulent, insistent, plaintive, and soft with entreaty" (*CW*, 946). Edna experiences plaintive needs and insistent longings. Music alone fills the room and parallels these feelings.

Music is heard everywhere in *The Awakening*. When Robert surprises Edna, the piano "strikes a discordant tone," and when he sings to her the "whole refrain haunted her memory." Victor sings, Mariequita hums, the boaters sing, and on the shore the hotel guests sing. Adèle plays the piano, and the Farival twins play duets. Music infuses the atmosphere and is even in the characters' thoughts. For example, Edna recalls the children as a "delicious song" when she travels home after visiting them at their grandmother's. As the narrative develops the music grows more mournful to foreshadow Edna's destiny.

In the screenplay I use music to highlight the action, retaining many of Chopin's sources, ranging from the classical pieces of Frédéric Chopin to popular local folk ballads. It is Mlle Reisz who plays Chopin during her several impromptu concerts, which take place when Edna experiences pensive moods. I use the song "Ah! Si Tu Savais" [If You Only Knew], as Chopin does, as a refrain of Edna's thoughts of Robert.

Even with all of Chopin's insistent musical touches the transposition from novel to screenplay requires significant additional musical resources. I relied on late nineteenth-century American composers and certain contemporary music that draws on women's heritage. The screenplay refers to Louis Moreau Gottschalk's "La Bamboula," a classical interpretation of the life of Congo Square, and to his "Tarantelle" during the night swimming party scene.[58] Gottschalk's music was well known for its sensual charm. Mortimer Wilson's festive "New Orleans," based on Mardi Gras, is my choice for the fast-paced scene at the racetrack. For additional flavor of the rich Louisiana musical heritage I include Theodore Von La Hace's "By the Banks of the River" to introduce Edna's reverie of her trip to Chênière Caminada. John Beach's "Orleans Alley," a turn-of-the-century impression of the city and its early morning street cries, is the background for the scene on the Pontellier veranda as Edna sees Léonce off, then retreats into inner reflection. I rely on the piano primarily because it was the main instrument of the era: "On the piano, composers from all walks of life expressed the events of the day."[59] A gramophone is placed in Edna's atelier to convey a further natural site for musical accompaniment. The melody referred to when Edna works in her studio, Ernest Guiraud's "Sylvia," had drifted down to her earlier on a walk through the streets; it recapitulates her inner wanderings.

In the scenes that prefigure the future I use contemporary music. In the birth scenes, Kay Gardner's "Mooncircles" provides an almost mythic commentary to the action. A well-known composer, Gardner has done considerable research on the historical record of women's music, which includes music to celebrate rituals of women's lives, such as childbirth. Some women's music, Gardner notes, is circular in form, patterned on a "ten-lunar-month" period, paralleling the time from conception to parturition. She also discusses how nature provides inspiration for women's music.[60] These ideas appear to mirror Chopin's own narrative intent.

Music and sound patterns enrich Edna's complex exploration of the inner self. The screenplay attempts to amplify these significant background aural harmonies. As Edna searches the streets of New Orleans a cacophony of sounds surrounds her, calls to her, evades her, follows her, disturbs her, and above all, provides a haunting reminder of the pervasive hold of culture on her.

An analysis of one all-important scene rounds out this discussion of interpretive strategies in adaptation as criticism. It is in the sea, as I have indicated, that Edna experiences her most powerful moments of authenticity and resolution, of which the suicide scene is the culmination. In the screenplay I follow Chopin's perspective that life is contradictory and unknowable, and that compromise is flawed. The meaning of the final scene continues to perplex readers and is the event in the novel on which scholars hold the most contradictory views. Chopin, I believe, intended the scene to have multiple meanings in that Edna's suicide is both an ironic statement on women's limited choices and a symbolic act of regeneration.

The first, and still germane, revelation about the scene lies in Kolodny's discussion of inversion, which she defines as the tendency to transpose generalized traditional images and conventional iconographic associations so that they come to connote their opposite. This idea is traced in *The Awakening:*

> There, the heroine, Edna Pontellier, feels herself "like some new born creature" at the very moment she is about to commit suicide; and, as she swims further out into the water, in the closing paragraphs, she thinks of it as "the bluegrass meadow that she traversed when a little child, believing that it had no beginning and no end." The imagery here, like the story line, is utilized to deny the conventional wisdom that swimming towards one's death is necessarily a dreary defeat of some kind of sinful or depressing termination.

Edna's pleasure, upon which critics of *The Awakening* frequently remark, occurs because "Edna has escaped to a higher realm."[61]

In one of many interpretations of this scene Gilbert finds it a "powerful metaphor of an angry snub at society." She reminds readers that Edna's suicide is untypical of other fictional heroines who choose death as an escape from misery. Edna turns her back on her world and swims "not into death but back into her own life, back into her own vision." Connecting Edna to the legend of Aphrodite Gilbert finds that she is journeying into a "regenerative and revisionary genre, a genre that intends to propose new realities for women by providing new mythic paradigms through which women's lives can be understood." Finally, in a reading she presents half-jestingly and calls hyperbolic, Gilbert asks, How do we ever know Edna dies? When last seen she is still swimming.[62]

Chopin's use of the sea as a site of Edna's quest is not uncommon: "In the voyage to subterranean or subaqueous territory, the heroine often emerges water-logged or weakened to the point of despair."[63]

When Edna first learns to swim "she seemed to be reaching out for the unlimited in which to lose herself" (*CW,* 908). Later when she converses at the cottages with Victor and Mariequita, who warn her of the water's chill, she responds: "Why it seems to me the sun is hot enough to have warmed the very depths of the ocean" (*CW,* 998–99). Where the sun is, life is, Chopin suggests.

On the beach Edna unashamedly sheds her bathing costume, the "unpleasant, pricking garments" (*CW,* 1,000). The gradual loosening of her clothes in earlier scenes prepares the reader for this moment, the "casting off" that is a symbol of Edna's "becoming her real self." There are none of the voyeuristic or lascivious attitudes that traditionally accompany women's nudity, and there are no false poses, lowered eyes, or modest gazes. Edna stands proud and natural in the open air as the sun envelops her with warmth.

The imagery of Edna's last moments—"the bees, spurs, and pinks"—can be better understood by relating similar imagery in Chopin's other stories. In "An Egyptian Cigarette," a character says, "I am going to the great city where men swarm like bees" (*CW,* 572), as an instance of longing for the "beyond" and to escape "fetters." In several stories the "hum of bees" accompanies death, but only as a completion of a responsibility or the end of a full life (*CW,* 410, 563). The bees and the pinks hint of the future, of the power of nature to disrupt man's civilization; by taking Edna to the beyond, they provide the link to a natural women's culture. The spurs are reference to men's domination of animals and symbolize the same male authority that causes Edna's struggle.

Edna says she feels "[l]ike some new-born creature" (*CW,* 1,000). To Edna the sea is a close embrace beyond the reach of an unjust tradition. The full blossoming of her inner self cannot emerge because compromise is essential for survival and because culture has failed to articulate alternatives. The suicide denies her country's myth of unlimited access to self-realization for the individual. In reality, self-realization is a male prerogative. The Victorian myth of love as the resolution of women's needs requires the submission of the self. Edna's decision both exposes the exclusiveness of the U.S. myth of independence and dismisses the romantic myth. Entrapped and doubly restricted by patriarchy, Edna is not only bound by the conventions of women's place but also therefore prohibited from participating in the masculine motif of self-discovery through venturing forth in the unlimited realms of land or sea. She must conduct her own quest in the space of mental and emotional interiority. In herself she seeks the adventure of discovery; she plants the seeds of the future within herself.

Some readers will question my decision to retain Chopin's final scene, now that women in the late twentieth century have so many more choices. It is not, to be wry, an issue of Edna enrolling in law school, but rather a belief in the power of Chopin's metaphor. Chopin's theme is ultimately about accommodation, about compromise. Through Edna Chopin poses a question few dare to ask, even today. Caught between claims of patriarchy and yearnings for autonomy, where do women turn? To invoke Marguerite Duras: "Duras has succeeded in making her films with the sure sense that we cannot simply jump out of masculine discourse and think up a woman who would somehow exist outside of the patriarchy."[64] The search for women's autonomy involves a reality in which neither biology, nor law, nor custom restricts the harmonious existence of the individual woman. It is a self that will be known when women's history is recovered, when social restraints are lifted, and when new paradigms are both intuited and reasoned. Until then, it is experimental to ask what constitutes an authentic woman. As Edna says: "I can't make it more clear, it's only something which I am beginning to comprehend, which is revealing itself to me" (CW, 929).

To suggest that Edna's quest is part of a continuum and that her refusal to accept the choices available to her is a particularly modern dilemma, I end the screenplay with a scene that is ambiguous yet suggests the theme. The Ratignolles are emblematic of the culture. While the appearance of Adèle's newborn baby is personal, the child also represents the new generation, the continuum. The future is unknowable. Time simply moves forward while change occurs steadily from generation to generation.

On the surface Kate Chopin followed the route of a traditional woman, devoted daughter, wife, and mother, her known rebellions confined to small acts of defiance—smoking, unconventional attire, walking about alone. Chopin's more daring departures from the female code of behavior, such as a probable love affair, as discovered by Toth, did not alter her circumstances. The turning point came in the wake of grief and uncertainty: in the aftermath of her husband's and mother's deaths, she embarked on a career as an author. From the beginning she wrote stories on the theme of women's inequality that are pure gems of characterization. As her stories sold and her reputation grew Chopin's fictional rebellion became more pronounced. In 1899, on the cusp of the new century and before the dawning of the "new woman," she published *The Awakening*. The novel's history of condemnation, neglect, and rediscovery in a way parallels recurrent eras in feminist history. Chopin's legacy has endured and now reaches the hearts and minds of contemporary women and men who share a ceaseless quest with her: the discovery of women's unfettered autonomy, which is for us all. As Edna says: "I know I shall like it, like the feeling of freedom and independence."

NOTES

Backgrounds

1. Leslie Garis, "Translating Fowler Into Film," 54.

2. Marilyn Hoder-Salmon, "The Intimate Agony of Mary McDougal Axelson's *Life Begins*," 55-69. Axelson came to Hollywood expecting to write the screenplay and was bitterly disappointed when director James Flood assigned the script to Earl Baldwin. She settled in Hollywood to establish herself as a scenarist, but eventually returned East.

3. Leslie Fiedler, *Love and Death in the American Novel*, 26; Molly Haskell, *From Reverence to Rape: The Treatment of Women in the Movies*, 61.

4. Kate Ellis, "Life with Marmee: Three Versions," 66.

5. Geoffrey Wagner, *The Novel and the Cinema*, 256.

6. Stanley Kauffmann, "Effi Briest," 20.

7. Joan Mellen, *Women and Their Sexuality in the New Film*, 21; Laura Mulvey, "Visual Pleasure and Narrative Cinema," 18; Claire Johnston, ed., "Critical Strategies," 4. For an overview on feminist film criticism there are several excellent recent collections; I particularly recommend Patricia Eren's *Issues in Feminist Film Criticism*. A superb bibliography appears in *Camera Obscura* 20-21 (1990): 336-77.

8. Lucy Fischer, *Shot/Countershot: Film Tradition and Women's Cinema*, 4; Judith Mayne, *The Woman at the Keyhole: Feminism and Women's Cinema*, 91.

9. Ruby Rich, "In the Name of Feminist Film Criticism," 238; Wood, "Images and Women," 334.

10. These works include Hugo Münsterberg's *The Film; A Psychological Study*; John Howard Lawson's *Theory and Technique of Playwriting and Screenwriting*; George Bluestone's *Novel into Film*; André Bazin's *What Is Cinema?*; Christian Metz's *Film Language: A Semiotics of the Cinema*; and Robert Richardson's *Literature and Film*.

11. Marsha Kinder, "Establishing A Discipline for the Teaching of Film: Criticism and the Literary Analogue," 425.

12. Dean Wilson Hartley, "How Do We Teach It?: A Primer for the Basic Literature/Film Course," 63; Joseph A. Gomez, *Ken Russell: The Adapter as Creator*, 27.

13. Regina K. Fadiman, *Faulkner's "Intruder in the Dust": Novel into Film*, vii, 4; Robert E. Morseberger and Katherine M. Morseberger, "Screenplay as Literature: Bibliography and Criticism," 47.

14. Paul Tiessen and Miguel Mota, "Re-writing Fitzgerald: Malcolm Lowry's *Tender Is the Night*," 31, 33.

15. Joy Gould Boyum, *Double Exposure: Fiction into Film*, 270.

16. Dudley Andrew, "The Well-Worn Muse: Adaptation in Film History and Theory," 10, 13.

17. Ibid., 14–15; Eric Rentschler, ed., *German Film and Literature* (London: Methuen, 1986), 5.

18. Jeffrey Sconce, "Narrative Authority and Social Narrativity: The Cinematic Reconstruction of Brontë's *Jane Eyre*," 48; Maureen Turim, "Gentlemen Consume Blondes," 109; Mark Graham, "The Proust Screenplay: *Temps perdu* for Harold Pinter," 51.

19. Thomas Duncan Anderson, "*Light in August*: Novel, Chamber Theater, Motion Pictures—The Role of Point of View in the Adaptation Process," 19, 17–18.

20. Mary Papke, *Verging on the Abyss: The Social Fiction of Kate Chopin and Edith Wharton*, 4.

21. Ibid., 61. See Daniel S. Rankin, *Kate Chopin and Her Creole Stories*; Per Seyersted, ed., *Kate Chopin: A Critical Biography*; and Emily Toth, *Kate Chopin: A Life of the Author of "The Awakening."* Toth's biography was not yet published when I wrote this study. Fortunately, I have been able to rely on her comprehensive study during final revisions to make certain that factual information about Kate Chopin corresponds with Toth's thoroughly researched findings, some of which alter previous Chopin lore. All Chopin critics are indebted to Toth for her devotion to Kate Chopin and to her legacy.

22. Rankin, *Kate Chopin*, 11.

23. Toth, *Kate Chopin*, 63–64.

24. Kate Chopin, *The Complete Works of Kate Chopin*, 897 (subsequent citations will appear parenthetically in the text as *CW*).

25. Per Seyersted and Emily Toth, *A Kate Chopin Miscellany*, 136.

26. Nancy Gehman and Nancy Ries, *Women and New Orleans*, 25–26.

27. Toth, *Kate Chopin*, 161.

28. Ibid., 10; and see also 163–75.

29. *CW*, "Confidence," 700. Later rewritten and published as "In the Confidence of a Story-Writer."

30. Seyersted, *Kate Chopin*, 58–59.

31. William Schuyler, "Kate Chopin," 116–17; Seyersted, *Kate Chopin,* 25.

32. Rankin, *Kate Chopin,* 72.

33. Seyersted, *Kate Chopin,* 54–55, 68–70.

34. Caroline Merrick, *Old Times in Dixieland,* 22–23.

35. In 1854 Margaret Fuller wrote *Women in the Nineteenth Century,* and John Stuart Mill followed in 1869 with *The Subjugation of Women.* In 1895 Elizabeth Cady Stanton's *The Woman's Bible* and Charlotte Perkins Gilman's *Woman and Economics* in 1898 were added to the list of the century's literature on inequality.

36. There is a revival of interest in *At Fault.* Bernard John Koloski in his dissertation, "Kate Chopin and the Search for a Code of Behavior" (University of Arizona 1972), takes the position that critical opinion that regards the novel as having a "weak structure" overlooks *At Fault's* themes, which are about disorder. Koloski claims that in this case, structure complements the theme. My own view is that *At Fault* offers a complex and illuminating view of such American issues as the dialectic between nature and technology and the forces between the North and the South during the post–Civil War era. Chopin's other known novel, *Young Dr. Gosse,* written in 1890, was never published. Chopin destroyed the manuscript.

37. A selection of the contemporary reviews are included in Margaret Culley, ed., *Norton Critical Edition of "The Awakening."* I quote from *The Mirror,* 4 May 1899; *Literature,* 23 June 1899; *Public Opinion,* 22 June 1899; *Chicago Times Herald,* 1 June 1899; and the *Los Angeles Sunday Times,* 25 June 1899.

38. *The Nation,* August 1899, 96. Other examples are given in an essay by Margaret Culley in *The Kate Chopin Newsletter,* 1 (Fall 1975): 28–29. As recently as 1974 a critic claimed that "Edna puts on a *bathing suit* [emphasis added] and swims to her death" (Ernest Earnest, *The American Eve in Fact and Fiction, 1775–1914* [Urbana: University of Illinois Press, 1974], 263), when even the most casual reading of the novel reveals the pronounced metaphor of casting off, which reaches its penultimate moment in the carefully detailed last scene as Edna "stand[s] naked under the sky!" (*CW,* 1000). Anthony Garitta traces the history of Chopin's literary reputation in relation to the criticism and social history in his dissertation, "The Critical Reputation of Kate Chopin" (University of North Carolina, 1982).

39. Also documented in Sidney Kramer's *A History of Stone & Kimball and Herbert S. Stone & Company* (Chicago: University of Chicago Press, 1940), 297.

40. Seyersted and Toth, *A Kate Chopin Miscellany,* 137.

41. There are numerous ironies related to its having been a Frenchman who set *The Awakening* on the path to rediscovery. For example, a St. Louis newspaper reporter who knew Chopin and called her "the Olive Schreiner of America" wrote that had she written in French "her books today [1911] would have been French classics." He noted that it required an intuitive culture to appreciate her gift and wisdom (*St. Louis Mirror,* 20 July 1911, 5–6).

42. Seyersted, *Kate Chopin,* 198.

43. Articles from the era of *The Awakening*'s rediscovery include Kenneth Eble's "A Forgotten Novel: Kate Chopin's *The Awakening*," 262, and Lewis Leary's "Kate Chopin, Liberationist?," in *Southern Literary Journal* 3 (1970): 139-44.

44. Joyce Ruddel Ladenson, "Rebellion Against Victorian Womanhood in Kate Chopin's *The Awakening*," 53.

45. Annette Kolodny, "Some Notes on Defining A 'Feminist Literary Criticism,'" 81; see also 82.

46. Eliane Jasenas, "The French Influence in Kate Chopin's *The Awakening*," 315, 319.

47. Jean Wyatt, *Reconstructing Desire: The Role of the Unconscious in Women's Reading and Writing*, 78-79; Marianne DeKoven, "Gendered Doubleness and the 'Origins' of Modernist Form," 20-21.

48. In recent times the cinematic qualities of Chopin's fiction have not gone unnoticed. For example, two short films of her short story "The Story of an Hour" have been made, one with the same title and the other called "The Joy that Kills," and they are frequently shown in feminist literature courses. A brief verbatim excerpt from *The Awakening* was made by Children's Television International for a university project, and there is also a version titled "The End of Summer"; more significantly, the Ted Turner network has plans to release a feature film called *Grand Isle* in fall 1992.

Interpretation

1. James Belson, "Maps of Consciousness: Creating an Inner Life for Character in Film and Novel," 235.

2. George Arms, "Kate Chopin's *The Awakening* in the Perspective of Her Literary Career," 217; Jane Tompkins, "*The Awakening*: An Evaluation," 24-25.

3. Otis Wheeler, "The Five Awakenings of Edna Pontellier," 122-23.

4. Toth, "Timely and Timeless: The Treatment of Time in *The Awakening* and *Sister Carrie*," 273; Alain Robbe-Grillet, *Last Year at Marienbad*, 9.

5. Robert Arner, "Music from a Farther Room: A Study of the Fiction of Kate Chopin," 114, 277.

6. Virginia Kouidis, "Prism into Prism: Emerson's 'Many-Colored Lenses' and the Woman Writer of Early Modernism," 118.

7. Eble, "A Forgotten Novel," 265; Carol Merrill, "Impressionism in Kate Chopin's *The Awakening*," 51; Sandra M. Gilbert, "The Second Coming of Aphrodite," 94.

8. Daniel M. Mendelowitz, *A History of American Art*, 307; Michael Gilmore, "Revolt against Nature," 64.

9. Arner, "Music from a Farther Room," 263.

10. Gilmore, "Revolt Against Nature," 64, 65.

11. Griselda Pollock, *Mary Cassatt*, 10, 27, 7.

12. Margit Stange, "Personal Property: Exchange Value and the Female Self in *The Awakening*," 107.

13. Roud, "Going Between," 159.

14. Mellen, *Women and Their Sexuality*, 54.

15. Annis Pratt, *Archetypal Patterns in Women's Fiction*, 11.

16. Charles Dudley Warner, "New Orleans," 310; John S. Kendall, "The French Quarter Sixty Years Ago," 91. Texts I used to develop background include Mark Twain's *Life on the Mississippi* and Robert Bush's *Grace King of New Orleans: A Selection of Her Writings*.

17. Truman Capote, *Music for Chameleons*, 194.

18. Henry Wikoff, *From the Reminiscences of an Idler*, 52; Lady Duffus Hardy, *Down South*, 241.

19. Joy L. Jackson, *New Orleans in the Gilded Age*, 10

20. Eleanor Early, *New Orleans Holiday*, 146.

21. Ibid., 98–99.

22. Kendall, "The French Quarter," 92.

23. Early, *New Orleans Holiday*, 146.

24. Hardy, *Down South*, 241.

25. Early, *New Orleans Holiday*, 239.

26. Fremont, *Souvenirs of My Time*, 177.

27. Seyersted, *Kate Chopin*, 151.

28. Carolyn Ramsey, *Cajuns On the Bayous*, 114.

29. Lafcadio Hearn, *Chita*, 22.

30. Rankin, *Kate Chopin*, 90.

31. Orrick Johns, "The 'Cadians,'" in *A Kate Chopin Miscellany*, ed. Seyersted and Toth, 153–54.

32. Gilbert, "Second Coming of Aphrodite," 96.

33. Anaïs Nin, *Anaïs Nin Reader*, 309, 311; Grace Stewart, *A New Mythos: The Novel of the Artist as Heroine, 1877–1977*, 178; Sharon Spencer, *Collage of Dreams: The Writings of Anaïs Nin*, 257; Kolodny, "Some Notes," 82.

34. Bernard Pinquad, "The Aquarium," 139.

35. Jackson, *New Orleans*, 255–57.

36. Dale A. Somers, *The Rise of Sports in New Orleans, 1850–1900*, 234, 144.

37. Annis Pratt, "Women and Nature in Modern Fiction," 488.

38. Stewart, *A New Mythos*, 108, 24.

39. Warner, "New Orleans," 311.

40. Kolodny, "Some Notes," 80–82; Carroll Smith-Rosenberg, "The Female World of Love and Ritual: Relations Between Women in Nineteenth-Century America," 1–29.

41. Cynthia Griffin Wolff, "Thanatos and Eros: Kate Chopin's *The Awakening*," 463.

42. Love restricted to the imagination is a recurring theme in Chopin's oeuvre. Lawrence Thornton also comments on Edna's psychological withdrawal from the seduction scene in "Edna as Icarus: A Mythic Issue" in Bernard Koloski, ed., *Approaches to Teaching Chopin's "The Awakening,"* 140.

43. Irene Dixon Smith, "The Louisiana Creole in Fiction," 533.

44. Ibid.

45. Anna Shannon Elfenbein, *Women on the Color Line: Evolving Stereotypes and the Writings of George Washington Cable, Grace King, Kate Chopin,* 148, 147.

46. Arner, "Music from a Farther Room," 169; Tompkins, *"The Awakening,"* 26; Helene E. Roberts, "Exquisite Slave: The Role of Clothes in the Making of the Victorian Woman," 557; Peter James Petersen, "The Fiction of Kate Chopin," 239.

47. Arner, "Music from a Farther Room," 59.

48. Ibid., 170.

49. Linda Nochlin, *Woman as Sex Object,* 74.

50. Harnett T. Kane, *Queen New Orleans: City by the River,* 32.

51. Alain Robbe-Grillet, *For a New Novel: Essays on Fiction,* 149; Roud, "Going Between," 159; Gomez, *Ken Russell,* 80, 112.

52. Jasenas, "The French Influence," 321.

53. I'm indebted to Robert Arner for this insight. There are many other examples in the novel, such as the exchange between Edna and Robert of "thought," "tired," and "August" (919): "stay" (910); "go" and "sun" (919); and the repetition of phrases such as "You were less fortunate than Robert, then," and "I am always less fortunate than Robert" (986).

54. Kolodny, "Some Notes," 79. An important early study is Robin Lakoff's *Language and Women's Place.* In recent studies I recommend *Linguistic Sex Roles in Conversation: Social Variation in the Expression of Tentativeness in English* by Brent Preisler (New York: Mouton de Gruyter, 1986).

55. Wyatt, *Reconstructing Desire,* 69.

56. Joan Clatworthy, "Kate Chopin: The Inward Life Which Questions," 194–95.

57. Arner, "Music from a Farther Room," 171–72.

58. Alfred Einstein, *Music in the Romantic Era.*

59. John Baron, *Piano Music from New Orleans, 1851–1898,* 12–14.

60. Kay Gardner, "Women's Composition," 163–77.

61. Kolodny, "Some Notes," 81, 82.

62. Gilbert, "Second Coming of Aphrodite," 104.

63. Stewart, *A New Mythos,* 109.

64. Susan H. Légar, "Marguerite Duras's Cinematic Spaces," 254.

SELECTED
BIBLIOGRAPHY

Abel, Elizabeth, Marianne Hirsch, and Elizabeth Langland, eds. *The Voyage In: Fictions of Female Development.* Hanover, N.H.: University Press of New England, 1983.

American Guide Series: New Orleans City Guide. Federal Writers' Project of the Works Progress Administration. Boston: Houghton Mifflin, 1938.

American Quarterly. "Special Issue: Film and American Studies" 31, no. 5 (1979).

Ammons, Elizabeth. *Conflicting Stories: American Women Writers at the Turn into the Twentieth Century.* New York: Oxford University Press, 1991.

Anderson, Thomas Duncan. "*Light In August*: Novel, Chamber Theater, Motion Picture—The Role of Point of View in the Adaptation Process." Ph.D. diss., Southern Illinois University, 1973.

Andrew, Dudley. "The Well-Worn Muse: Adaptation in Film History and Theory," in *Narrative Strategies: Original Essays in Film and Prose Fiction,* edited by Syndy M. Conger and Janice R. Welsch, 11–17. Macomb: Western Illinois University Press, 1980.

Arms, George. "Kate Chopin's *The Awakening* in the Perspective of Her Literary Career." In *Essays in American Literature in Honor of Jay B. Hubbell,* edited by Clarence Gohdes, 215–28. Durham, N.C.: Duke University Press, 1967.

Arner, Robert. "Music from a Farther Room: A Study of the Fiction of Kate Chopin." Ph.D. diss., Pennsylvania State University, 1970. Also published as a special issue, *Louisiana Studies* 14, no. 1 (Spring 1975).

Auerbach, Nina. *Women and the Demon.* Cambridge, Mass.: Harvard University Press, 1982.

Baron, John. *Piano Music From New Orleans, 1851–1898.* Music Reprint Series. New York: Da Capo, 1980.

Basch, Norma. "Invisible Women: The Legal Fiction of Marital Unity in Nineteenth-Century America." *Feminist Studies* 5, no. 2 (1979): 346–65.

Basso, Etolia S., ed. *The World From Jackson Square: A New Orleans Reader.* New York: Farrar, Straus, 1948.

Bauer, Dale M. *Feminist Dialogics: A Theory of Failed Community.* Albany: State University of New York Press, 1988.

Bazin, André. *What is Cinema?* Translated by Hugh Gray. 2 vols. Berkeley: University of California Press, 1967, 1971.

Bellony-Rewald, Alice. *The Lost World of the Impressionists.* Boston: New York Graphic Society, 1976.

Belson, James Ira. "Maps of Consciousness: Creating an Inner Life for Character in Film and Novel." Ph.D. diss., University of Southern California, 1973.

Bender, Bert. "Kate Chopin's Lyrical Short Stories." *Studies In Short Fiction* 2, no. 3 (1974): 257–66.

Benstock, Shari. *Feminist Issues in Literary Scholarship.* Bloomington: Indiana University Press, 1987.

Berggren, Paula. "A Lost Soul: Work Without Hope in *The Awakening.*" *Regionalism and the Female Imagination* 3, no. 1 (1977): 1–8.

Bergman, Ingmar. *Four Screenplays.* Translated by Lars Malmstrom and David Kushner. New York: Simon and Schuster, 1960.

Bluestone, George. *Novels into Film.* Berkeley and Los Angeles: University of California Press, 1957.

Bonner, Thomas, Jr. *The Kate Chopin Companion: With Chopin's Translations from French Fiction.* Westport, Conn.: Greenwood, 1988.

Boyle, Richard T. *American Impressionism.* Boston: New York Graphic Society, 1976.

Boyum, Joy Gould. *Double Exposure: Fiction Into Film.* New York: New American Library, 1985.

Bridaham, Lester Burbank, ed. *New Orleans and Bayou Country: Photographs (1880–1910) by George François Mugnier.* New York: Weathervane, 1962.

Bush, Robert, ed. *Grace King of New Orleans: A Selection of Her Writings.* Baton Rouge: Louisiana State University Press, 1973.

Cable, Mary. *Lost New Orleans.* Boston: Houghton Mifflin Company, 1980.

Camera Obscura: A Journal of Feminism and Film Theory. Series, Fall 1977–Fall 1990.

Capote, Truman. *Music for Chameleons.* New York: Random House, 1980.

Capote, Truman, Eleanor Perry, and Frank Perry. *Trilogy: An Experiment in Multimedia.* New York: Macmillan, 1969.

Chatman, Seymour. *Story and Discourse: Narrative Structure in Fiction and Film.* Ithaca, N.Y.: Cornell University Press, 1978.

Chopin, Kate. *At Fault.* St. Louis: Nixon-Jones Printing Company, 1890.

———. *The Complete Works of Kate Chopin.* 2 vols. Edited by Per Seyersted. Baton Rouge: Louisiana State University Press, 1969.

————. Copies of letters and poems. Missouri Historical Society, St. Louis.

————. "In the Confidence of a Story-Writer." *Atlantic Monthly* 83 (January 1899): 137–39.

Christ, Carol P. *Diving Deep and Surfacing: Women Writers on Spiritual Quest.* Boston: Beacon Press, 1981.

Christovich, Mary Louise. *The Esplanade Ridge.* Vol. 5 of *New Orleans Architecture.* Gretna, La.: Pelican, 1977.

Clatworthy, Joan Mayerson. "Kate Chopin: The Inward Life which Questions." Ph.D. diss., State University of New York at Buffalo, 1979.

Cocke, Edward J. *Monumental New Orleans.* Photographs, Robert Brown. New Orleans: Lafayette, 1968.

Cohen, Keith. *Film and Fiction: The Dynamics of Exchange.* New Haven, Conn.: Yale University Press, 1979.

Colby, Vineta. *The Singular Anomaly: Women Novelists of the Nineteenth Century.* New York: New York University Press, 1970.

Collins, Robert. "The Dismantling of Edna Pontellier: Garment Imagery in Kate Chopin's *The Awakening.*" *Southern Studies* 23 (Summer 1984): 176–97.

Cornwell, Regina. "Maya Deren and Germaine Dulac: Activists of the Avant-Garde." *Film Library Quarterly* 5, no. 1 (1971–72): 29–36.

Cott, Nancy F. "Passionless: An Interpretation of Victorian Sexist Ideology, 1790–1890." *Signs* 4, no. 2 (1978): 219–36.

Craven, Avery O. *Rachel of Old Louisiana.* Baton Rouge: Louisiana State University Press, 1975.

Culley, Margaret, ed. *"The Awakening": An Authoritative Text, Contexts, Criticism.* New York: Norton, 1976.

Davies, Mel. "Corsets and Conception: Fashion and Demographic Trends in the Nineteenth Century." In *Comparative Studies in Society and History,* edited by Raymond Grew and Eric R. Wolf, 611–41. New York: Cambridge University Press, 1982.

Deer, Irving. "Strindberg's Dream Vision: Prelude to the Film." *Criticism* 14, no. 3 (1972): 253–65.

DeKoven, Marianne. "Gendered Doubleness and the 'Origins' of Modernist Form." *Tulsa Studies in Women's Literature* 8, no. 1 (Spring 1989): 19–42.

De Lauretis, Teresa. *Technologies of Gender: Essays on Theory, Film, and Fiction.* Bloomington: Indiana University Press, 1987.

————, ed. *Feminist Studies/Critical Studies.* Bloomington: Indiana University Press, 1986.

Diamond, Arlyn, and Lee R. Edwards, eds. *The Authority of Experience: Essays in Feminist Criticism.* Amherst: University of Massachusetts Press, 1977.

Doane, Mary Ann, Patricia Mellencamp, and Linda Williams, eds. *Revisions: Essays in Feminist Film Criticism.* Frederick, Md.: University Publications of America and the American Film Institute, 1984.

Dowling, Linda. "The Decadent and the New Woman in the 1890's." *Nineteenth Century Fiction* 33, no. 4 (1979): 434–53.

Early, Eleanor. *New Orleans Holiday.* New York: Rinehart, 1947.

Eble, Kenneth. "A Forgotten Novel: Kate Chopin's *The Awakening.*" *Western Humanities Review* 10 (1956): 261–69.

Ecker, Gisela, ed. *Feminist Aesthetics.* Translated by Harriet Anderson. Boston: Beacon, 1985.

Edwards, Lee R. *Psyche as Hero: Female Heroism and Fictional Form.* Middletown, Conn.: Wesleyan University Press, 1984.

Eidsvik, Charles. *Cineliteracy.* New York: Random House, 1978.

——. "Toward a 'Politique des Adaptations.'" *Literature/Film Quarterly* 3, no. 3 (1975): 255–63.

Einstein, Alfred. *Music in the Romantic Era.* New York: Norton, 1947.

Eisenstein, Sergei. *Film Form.* Edited and translated by Jay Leyda. New York: Harcourt Brace & World, 1977.

——. *The Film Sense.* Edited and translated by Jay Leyda. New York: Praeger, 1947.

Elfenbein, Anna Shannon. *Women on the Color Line: Evolving Stereotypes and the Writings of George Washington Cable, Grace King, Kate Chopin.* Charlottesville: University Press of Virginia, 1989.

Ellis, Kate. "Life with Marmee: Three Versions." In *The Classic American Novel and the Movies,* edited by Gerald Peary and Roger Shatzkin, 62–72. New York: Ungar, 1977.

Erens, Patricia, ed. *Issues in Feminist Film Criticism.* Bloomington: Indiana University Press, 1990.

Ewell, Barbara C. *Kate Chopin.* New York: Unger, 1986.

Fadiman, Regina K. *Faulkner's "Intruder In the Dust": Novel into Film.* Knoxville: University of Tennessee Press, 1978.

Fell, John L. *Film and the Narrative Tradition.* Norman: University of Oklahoma Press, 1974.

Fenton, Jill Rubinson, Jane Russo, and Charles Waugh, eds. *Women Writers from Page to Screen.* New York: Garland, 1990.

Fetterley, Judith. *The Resisting Reader: A Feminist Approach to American Fiction.* Bloomington: Indiana University Press, 1978.

Fiedler, Leslie. *Love and Death in the American Novel.* New York: Stein and Day, 1966.

Fischer, Lucy. *Shot/Countershot: Film Tradition and Women's Cinema.* Princeton, N.J.: Princeton University Press, 1989.

Fitzhugh, Daisy. "Famous Beauties of the South." *Demorest's Family Magazine* 28, no. 1 (1891).

Fletcher, Marie. "The Southern Woman in the Fiction of Kate Chopin." *Louisiana History* 7, no. 2 (1966): 117–32.

Flynn, Elizabeth, and Patrocinio P. Schweickart, eds. *Gender and Reading: Essays on Readers, Texts, and Contexts.* Baltimore: Johns Hopkins University Press, 1986.

Foote, Horton. *The Screenplay of "To Kill A Mockingbird."* New York: Harcourt Brace & World, 1962.

Fremont, Jessie Benton. *Souvenirs of My Time.* Boston: D. Lothrop, 1887.

French, Brandon. *On The Verge of Revolt: Women in American Films of the Fifties.* New York: Ungar, 1978.

Froug, William. *The Screenwriter Looks at the Screenwriter.* New York: Macmillan, 1972.

Fryer, Judith. *The Faces of Eve: Women in the Nineteenth-Century American Novel.* New York: Oxford University Press, 1976.

Gaines, Jane. "Costume and Narrative: How Dress Tells the Woman's Story." In *Fabrications: Costume and the Female Body,* edited by Jane Gaines and Charlotte Herzog, 180–211. New York: Routledge, 1990.

Gardner, Kay. "Women's Composition." In *Women's Culture: The Renaissance of the Seventies,* edited by Gayle Kimball, 163–77. Metuchen, N.J.: Scarecrow, 1981.

Garis, Leslie. "Translating Fowler into Film." Interview with Harold Pinter. *New York Times Magazine,* 30 August 1981, 52–54.

Gaude, Pamela Parker. "*The Awakening:* A Study of Maupassant's Influence on Kate Chopin." *Revue de Louisiane* 4, no. 2 (1975): 19–27.

Geduld, Harry M., ed. *Authors on Film.* Bloomington: Indiana University Press, 1972.

Gehman, Mary, and Nancy Ries. *Women and New Orleans: A History.* New Orleans: Margaret Media, 1988.

Gelpi, Barbara, Nannerl Keohane, and Michelle Rosaldo, eds. *Feminist Theory: A Critique of Ideology.* Chicago: University of Chicago Press, 1982.

Gentile, Mary C. *Film Feminisms: Theory and Practice.* Westport, Conn.: Greenwood, 1985.

Gessner, Robert. *The Moving Image: A Guide to Cinematic Literacy.* New York: Dutton, 1968.

Giddings, Robert, Keith Selby and Chris Wensley. *Screening the Novel: The Theory and Practice of Literary Adaptation.* New York: St. Martins, 1990.

Gilbert, Sandra M. "The Second Coming of Aphrodite." In *Modern Critical Views: Kate Chopin,* edited by Harold Bloom, 89–114. New York: Chelsea House, 1987.

Gilmore, Michael. "Revolt Against Nature: The Problematic Modernism of *The Awakening.*" In *New Essays on "The Awakening,"* edited by Wendy Martin, 59–88. Cambridge: Cambridge University Press, 1988.

Gomez, Joseph A. *Ken Russell: The Adapter as Creator.* New York: Pergamon, 1977.

Graham, Mark. "The Proust Screenplay: *Temps perdu* for Harold Pinter." *Literature/Film Quarterly* 10, no. 1 (1982): 38–52.

Hardy, Lady Duffus. *Down South*. London: Chapman and Hall, 1883.

Harrington, John. *Film and/as Literature*. Englewood Cliffs, N.J.: Prentice-Hall, 1977.

Harris, Susan K. *Nineteenth-Century American Women's Novels*. New York: Cambridge University Press, 1990.

Hartley, Dean Wilson. "How Do We Teach It? A Primer for the Basic Literature/Film Course." *Literature/Film Quarterly* 3, no. 1 (1975): 60–79.

Haskell, Molly. *From Reverence to Rape: The Treatment of Women in the Movies*. 2d ed. Chicago: University of Chicago Press, 1987.

Hearn, Lafcadio. *Chita*. 1889. Reprint. Chapel Hill: University of North Carolina Press, 1969.

Heilbrun, Carolyn. *Reinventing Womanhood*. New York: Norton, 1979.

Hoder-Salmon, Marilyn. "The Intimate Agony of Mary McDougal Axelson's *Life Begins*." *American Studies* 18 (Winter 1978): 55–69.

Horton, Andrew, and Joan Magretta, eds. *Modern European Filmmakers and the Art of Adaptation*. New York: Ungar, 1981.

Huf, Linda. *A Portrait of the Artist as a Young Woman: The Writer as Heroine in American Literature*. New York: Ungar, 1983.

Jackson, Joy L. *New Orleans in the Gilded Age: Politics and Urban Progress, 1880–1896*. Baton Rouge: Louisiana State University Press, 1969.

Jasenas, Eliane. "The French Influence in Kate Chopin's *The Awakening*." *Nineteenth Century French Studies* 4, no. 3 (Spring 1976): 312–21.

Jinks, William. *The Celluloid Literature*. Beverly Hills, Calif.: Glencoe, 1971.

Johnston, Claire. "Critical Strategies in Dorothy Arzner." In *The Work of Dorothy Arzner: Towards a Feminist Cinema*, edited by Claire Johnston, 3–27. London: British Film Institute, 1975.

Jones, Ann Goodwyn. *Tomorrow is Another Day: The Woman Writer in the South, 1859–1936*. Baton Rouge: Louisiana State University Press, 1981.

Kane, Harnett T. *Plantation Parade: The Grand Manner in Louisiana*. New York: Bonanza, 1965.

———. *Queen New Orleans: City by the River*. New York: Bonanza, 1969.

Kauffmann, Stanley. "Effi Briest." *The New Republic* 26 (1977): 176.

Kay, Karyn, and Gerald Peary, eds. *Women and the Cinema: A Critical Anthology*. New York: Dutton, 1977.

Kendall, John S. "The French Quarter Sixty Years Ago." *Louisiana Historical Quarterly* 34, no. 2 (April 1951): 91–102.

———. "A New Orleans Lady of Letters." *Louisiana Historical Quarterly* 19, no. 2 (1936): 436–63.

Kinder, Marsha. "Establishing A Discipline for the Teaching of Film: Criticism and the Literary Analogue." *Quarterly Review of Film Studies* 1 (1976): 424–29.

King, Grace. *New Orleans: The Place and the People*. New York: Macmillan, 1934.

Kolodny, Annette. "'Dancing Through the Minefield': Some Observations on the Theory and Practice of Feminist Literary Criticism." *Feminist Studies* 6, no. 1 (1980): 1–25.

———. "Some Notes on Defining a 'Feminist Literary Criticism.'" *Critical Inquiry* 2 (Autumn 1975): 75–92.

Koloski, Bernard, ed. *Approaches to Teaching Chopin's "The Awakening."* New York: Modern Language Association of America, 1988.

Kouidis, Virginia M. "Prism Into Prism: Emerson's 'Many-Colored Lenses' and the Woman Writer of Early Modernism." In *The Green American Tradition: Essays and Poems for Sherman Paul*, edited by H. Daniel Peck, 115–34. Baton Rouge: Louisiana State University Press, 1989.

Kuhn, Annette. *Women's Pictures: Feminism and Cinema.* London: Routledge & Kegan Paul, 1982.

Ladenson, Joyce R. "Rebellion Against Victorian Womanhood in Kate Chopin's *The Awakening.*" *Intellect* 104, no. 2367 (July/August 1975): 52–55.

Lakoff, Robin. *Language and Women's Place.* New York: Harper & Row, 1975.

Lawson, John Howard. *Theory and Technique of Playwriting and Screenwriting.* New York: Putnam, 1936.

Légar, Susan H. "Marguerite Duras's Cinematic Spaces." In *Women and Film*, edited by Janet Todd, 231–57. New York: Holmes and Meier, 1988.

Levine, Robert S. "Circadian Rhythms and Rebellion in Kate Chopin's *The Awakening.*" *Studies in American Fiction* 10, no. 1 (Spring 1982): 71–81.

Linden, George W. *Reflections on the Screen.* Belmont, Calif.: Wadsworth, 1970.

Lippard, Lucy R. *Feminist Essays in Women's Art.* New York: Dutton, 1976.

Luhr, William, and Peter Lehman, eds. *Authorship and Narrative in the Cinema: Issues in Contemporary Aesthetics and Criticism.* Toms River, N.J.: Capricorn, 1977.

MacBean, James Roy. *Film and Revolution.* Bloomington: Indiana University Press, 1975.

MacCann, Richard Dyer. *Film: A Montage of Theories.* New York: Dutton, 1969.

McConnell, Frank D. "Film and Writing: The Political Dimension." *Massachusetts Review* 13, no. 4 (1978): 543–62.

———. *The Spoken Seen: Film and the Romantic Imagination.* Baltimore: Johns Hopkins University Press, 1975.

———. *Storytelling and Mythmaking: Images from Film and Literature.* New York: Oxford University Press, 1979.

McDougal, Stuart Y. *Made into Movies: From Literature to Film.* New York: Holt, Rinehart & Winston, 1985.

McVoy, Lizzie Carter, ed. *Louisiana in the Short Story.* Baton Rouge: Louisiana State University Press, 1940

Maddux, Rachel, Stirling Silliphant, and Neil D. Issacs. *Fiction into Film: "A Walk in the Spring Rain."* New York: Dell, 1970.

Manheimer, Joan. "Murderous Mothers: The Problem of Parenting in the Victorian Novel." *Feminist Studies* 5, no. 3 (1979): 530–46.

Marcus, Fred H. *Film and Literature: Contrasts in Media.* Scranton, Pa.: Chandler, 1971.

Martin, Wendy, ed. *New Essays on "The Awakening."* Cambridge: Cambridge University Press, 1988.

Mast, Gerald, and Marshall Cohen. *Film Theory and Criticism: Introductory Readings.* New York: Oxford University Press, 1974.

May, John R. "Local Color in *The Awakening.*" *Southern Review* 6 (1970): 1031–40.

Mayne, Judith. "Feminist Film Theory and Criticism." *Signs* 11, no. 1 (Autumn 1985): 81–100.

———. *Private Novels, Public Films.* Athens: University of Georgia Press, 1988.

———. *The Woman at the Keyhole: Feminism and Women's Cinema.* Bloomington: Indiana University Press, 1990.

Meese, Elizabeth A. *Crossing the Double-Cross: The Practice of Feminist Criticism.* Chapel Hill: University of North Carolina Press, 1986.

Mehring, Margaret. *The Screenplay: A Blend of Film Form and Content.* Boston: Focal, 1990.

Mellen, Joan. *Women and Their Sexuality in the New Film.* 1973. Reprint. New York: Dell, 1973.

Mendelowitz, Daniel M. *A History of American Art.* New York: Holt, Rinehart & Winston, 1973.

Merrick, Caroline. *Old Times in Dixieland.* New York: Grafton, 1901.

Merrill, Carol. "Impressionism in Kate Chopin's *The Awakening.*" *New America* 3, no. 2 (1977): 50–52.

Metz, Christian. *Film Language: A Semiotics of the Cinema.* Translated by Michael Taylor. New York: Oxford University Press, 1974.

Miller, Gabriel. *Screening the Novel: Rediscovered American Fiction in Film.* New York: Ungar, 1980.

Monaco, James. *How to Read a Film: The Art, Technology, Language, History and Theory of Film and Media.* New York: Oxford University Press, 1977.

Moreno, Julio L. "Subjective Cinema: And the Problems of Film in the First Person." *Quarterly of Film, Radio and Television* 7, no. 4 (1953): 341–58.

Morrissette, Bruce. *Novel and Film: Essays in Two Genres.* Chicago: University of Chicago Press, 1985.

Morseberger, Robert E., and Katherine M. Morseberger. "Screenplay As Literature: Bibliography and Criticism." *Literature/Film Quarterly* 3, no. 1 (1975): 45–59.

Mulvey, Laura. "Visual Pleasure and Narrative Cinema." *Screen* 16, no. 3 (Autumn 1975): 6–18.

Münsterberg, Hugo. *The Film: A Psychological Study.* 1916. Reprint. New York: Dover, 1969.

Murray, Edward. *The Cinematic Imagination: Writers and the Motion Pictures.* New York: Ungar, 1972.

Nichols, Bill, ed. *Movies and Methods.* Vol. 2. Berkeley: University of California Press, 1985.

Nin, Anaïs. *Anaïs Nin Reader.* Edited by Philip K. Jason. Chicago: Swallow, 1973.

———. "Poetics of the Film." *Film Culture* 30 (1963–64): 12–14.

Nobles, Katherine. "Some Distinguished New Orleans Women." *American Woman* 10, no. 5 (1894).

Nochlin, Linda. *Woman as Sex Object.* New York: Newsweek, 1972.

O'Donnell, Mary King. *Those Other People.* Boston: Houghton Mifflin, 1946.

Packard, William. *The Art of Scriptwriting.* New York: Paragon House, 1987.

Papke, Mary. *Verging on the Abyss: The Social Fiction of Kate Chopin and Edith Wharton.* Westport, Conn.: Greenwood, 1990.

Peary, Gerald, and Roger Shatzkin, eds. *The Classic American Novel and the Movies.* New York: Ungar, 1977.

Penley, Constance, ed. *Feminism and Film Theory.* New York: Routledge and Kegan Paul, 1988.

Petersen, Peter James. "The Fiction of Kate Chopin." Ph.D. diss., University of New Mexico, 1972.

Pinquad, Bernard. "The Aquarium." *Sight and Sound* 32, no. 3 (1963): 136–39.

Pollock, Griselda. *Mary Cassatt.* New York: Harper & Row, 1980.

Portnoy, Kenneth. *Screen Adaptation: A Scriptwriting Handbook.* Boston: Focal, 1991.

Poston, Carol S. "Childbirth in Literature." *Feminist Studies* 4, no. 2 (1978): 18–31.

Powdermaker, Hortense. *Hollywood: The Dream Factory.* Boston: Little, Brown, 1950.

Prats, A. T. *The Autonomous Image: Cinematic Narration and Humanism.* Lexington: University Press of Kentucky, 1981.

Pratt, Annis. *Archetypal Patterns in Women's Fiction.* Bloomington: Indiana University Press, 1981.

———. "Woman and Nature in Modern Fiction." *Contemporary Literature* 13, no. 4 (1972): 476–90.

Rabine, Leslie W. *Reading the Romantic Heroine: Text, History, Ideology.* Ann Arbor: University of Michigan Press, 1985.

Ramsey, Carolyn. *Cajuns on the Bayous.* New York: Hastings House, 1957.

Rankin, Daniel S. *Kate Chopin and Her Creole Stories.* Philadelphia: University of Pennsylvania Press, 1932.

Regionalism and the Female Imagination (formerly the *Kate Chopin Newsletter*). Complete series 1, no. 1 (1975) to 4, no. 3 (1979).

Rich, Ruby. "In the Name of Feminist Film Criticism." In *Issues in Feminist Film Criticism,* edited by Patricia Erens, 268–87. Bloomington: Indiana University Press, 1990.

Richardson, Robert. *Literature and Film*. Bloomington: Indiana University Press, 1969.

Ripley, Eliza. *Social Life in Old New Orleans: Being Recollections of my Girlhood*. New York: Appleton, 1912.

Robbe-Grillet, Alain. *For a New Novel: Essays on Fiction*. Translated by Richard Howard. New York: Grove, 1965.

———. *Last Year at Marienbad*. New York: Grove, 1962.

Roberts, Helene E. "The Exquisite Slave: The Role of Clothes in the Making of the Victorian Woman." *Signs* 2, no. 3 (1977): 554–69.

Robinson, Lura. *It's an Old New Orleans Custom*. New York: Bonanza, 1968.

Rollins, Peter C. "Film and American Studies: Questions, Activities, Guides." *American Quarterly* 26, no. 3 (1974): 245–65.

Rosowski, Susan J. "The Novel of Awakening." *Genre* 12 (1979): 313–32.

Roud, Richard. "Going Between." *Sight and Sound* 40, no. 3 (1971): 158–59.

Schuler, Kathryn Reinhart. "Women in Public Affairs in Louisiana During Reconstruction." *Louisiana Historical Quarterly* 19, no. 3 (1956): 668–750

Schuyler, William. "Kate Chopin." *Writer* 7 (August 1894): 115–17.

Sconce, Jeffrey. "Narrative Authority and Social Narrativity: The Cinematic Reconstruction of Brontë's *Jane Eyre*," *Wide Angle* 10, no. 1 (1988): 46–61

Seyersted, Per, ed. *Kate Chopin: A Critical Biography*. Baton Rouge: Louisiana State University Press, 1969.

Seyersted, Per, and Emily Toth, eds. *A Kate Chopin Miscellany*. Natchitoches, La.: Northwestern State University Press, 1979.

Shaw, Pat. "Putting Audience in Its Place: Psychosexuality and Perspective Shifts in *The Awakening*." *American Literary Realism, 1870–1910* 23, no. 1 (Fall 1990): 61–69.

Showalter, Elaine, ed. *Women, Literature, and Theory*. New York: Pantheon, 1985.

Silverstein, Norman, ed. "Film as Literature and Language." *Journal of Modern Literature* 3, no. 2 (1973).

Sinyard, Neal. *Filming Literature: The Art of Screen Adaptation*. New York: St. Martin's, 1986.

Sitney, P. Adams, ed. *Film Culture Reader*. New York: Praeger, 1970.

———. *Visionary Film*. New York: Oxford University Press, 1974.

Sklar, Robert. *Movie-Made America: A Cultural History of American Movies*. New York: Vintage, 1976.

Smith, Irene Dixon. "The Louisiana Creole in Fiction." Master's thesis, Tulane University, 1956.

Smith-Rosenberg, Carroll. "The Female World of Love and Ritual: Relations Between Women in Nineteenth-Century America." *Signs* 1, no. 1 (1975): 1–29.

Snyder-Ott, Joelynn. *Women and Creativity*. Milbrae, Calif.: Les Femmes, 1978.

Sochen, June. "Mildred Pierce and Women in Film." *American Quarterly* 30, no. 1 (1978): 3–20.

Somers, Dale A. *The Rise of Sports in New Orleans, 1850–1900.* Baton Rouge: Louisiana State University Press, 1972.

Spencer, Sharon. *Collage of Dreams: The Writings of Anaïs Nin.* Chicago: Swallow, 1978.

Spiegel, Alan. *Fiction and the Camera Eye: Visual Consciousness in Film and the Modern Novel.* Charlottesville: University Press of Virginia, 1976.

Stange, Margit. "Personal Property: Exchange Value and the Female Self in *The Awakening.*" *Genders* 5 (Summer 1989): 106–19.

Stevenson, Ralph, and J. R. Debrix. *The Cinema as Art.* London: Penguin, 1965.

Stewart, Grace. *A New Mythos: The Novel of the Artist as Heroine 1877–1977.* Montreal: Eden, 1979.

Swann, Dwight V. *Film Scriptwriting: A Practical Manual.* 2d ed. Boston: Focal, 1989.

Tallent, Robert. *The Romantic New Orleans.* New York: Dutton, 1950.

Taylor, Helen. *Gender, Race, and Region in the Writings of Grace King, Ruth McEnery Stuart, and Kate Chopin.* Baton Rouge: Louisiana State University Press, 1989.

Tiessen, Paul, and Miguel Mota. *The Cinema of Malcolm Lowry.* Vancouver: University of British Columbia Press, 1990.

———. "Re-writing Fitzgerald: Malcolm Lowry's *Tender is the Night.*" In *Transformation: From Literature to Film,* edited by Douglas Radcliff-Umsted, 30–35. Proceedings of the Fifth International Conference on Film, Kent State University, 1987.

Todd, Janet, ed. *Gender and Literary Voice: Women and Literature.* New York: Holmes and Meier, 1988.

———. *Women and Film.* New York: Holmes and Meier, 1988.

Tompkins, Jane P. "*The Awakening*: An Evaluation." *Feminist Studies* 3, no. 3/4 (1976): 22–29.

Toth, Emily. "The Cult of Domesticity and 'A Sentimental Soul.'" *Kate Chopin Newsletter* 1, no. 2 (1975): 9–16.

———. *Kate Chopin: A Life of the Author of The Awakening.* New York: Morrow, 1990.

———. "Timely and Timeless: The Treatment of Time in *The Awakening* and *Sister Carrie.*" *Southern Studies* 16, no. 3 (1977): 271–76.

Treichler, Paula A. "The Construction of Ambiguity in *The Awakening*: A Linguistic Analysis." In *Women and Language in Literature and Society,* edited by Sally McConnel-Ginet, Ruth Borker, and Nelly Furman, 239–57. New York: Praeger, 1980.

Turim, Maureen. "Gentlemen Consume Blondes." In *Issues in Feminist Film Crit-*

icism, edited by Patricia Erens, 101–11. Bloomington: Indiana University Press, 1990.

Twain, Mark. *Life on the Mississippi*. New York: Harper & Row, 1874.

Wagner, Geoffrey. *The Novel and the Cinema*. Cranbury, N.J.: Fairleigh Dickinson University Press, 1975.

Warner, Charles D. "New Orleans." *Harper's*, 74, no. 440 (January 1887).

Welch, Jeffrey Egan. *Literature and Film: An Annotated Bibliography, 1900–1977*. New York: Garland, 1981.

Welsch, Janice R. "Feminist Film Theory/Criticism in the United States." *Journal of Film and Video* 39 (Spring 1987): 66–81.

Wertmüller, Lina. *The Screenplays of Lina Wertmüller*. New York: Quadrangle, 1977.

Wheeler, Otis. "The Five Awakenings of Edna Pontellier." *Southern Review* 2 (January 1975): 118–28.

Wikoff, Henry. *From the Reminiscences of an Idler*. New York: Fords, Howard, and Hulbert, 1880.

Wilson, W. H. *The Diary of a Louisiana Woman*. Unpublished ms. Howard-Tilton Memorial Library, Tulane University.

Winston, Douglas Garrett. *The Screenplay as Literature*. New Jersey: Associated University Presses, Inc., 1973.

Wolff, Cynthia Griffin. "Thanatos and Eros: Kate Chopin's *The Awakening*." *American Quarterly* 25, no. 4 (October 1973): 449–71.

Wollen, Peter. *Signs and Meaning in the Cinema*. Bloomington: Indiana University Press, 1972.

Wyatt, Jean. *Reconstructing Desire: The Role of the Unconscious in Women's Reading and Writing*. Chapel Hill: University of North Carolina Press, 1990.

Yaeger, Patricia. *Honey-Mad Women: Emancipatory Strategies in Women's Writing*. New York: Columbia University Press, 1988.

INDEX

The screenplay, "Edna," pp. 29–105, has not been included in this index.

Library of Congress Cataloging-in-Publication Data

Hoder-Salmon, Marilyn, 1934–
    Kate Chopin's The awakening: screenplay as interpretation /
Marilyn Hoder-Salmon.
        p. cm.
    Includes bibliographical references and index.
    ISBN 0–8130–1136–1 (alk. paper)
    1. Chopin, Kate, 1851–1904. Awakening. 2. Chopin, Kate,
1851–1904—Film and video adaptations. 3. American fiction—Film
and video adaptations. I. Chopin, Kate, 1851–1904. Awakening.
II. Title.
PS1294.C63A6434   1992   92-3801
791.43′72—dc20   CIP